P9-EFI-983

Developing a GIVING CHURCH

BY
STAN TOLER AND
ELMER TOWNS

Beacon Hill Press of Kansas City
Kansas City, Missouri

Copyright 1999
by Beacon Hill Press of Kansas City

ISBN 083-411-7738

Printed in the United States of America

Cover Design: Michael Walsh

Library of Congress Cataloging-in-Publication Data
Towns, Elmer L.
   Developing a giving church / Elmer Towns, Stan Toler.
      p.   cm.
   Includes bibliographical references (p.   ).
   ISBN 0-8341-1773-8 (pbk.)
   1. Church fund raising.   I. Toler, Stan.   II. Title.
BV772.5.T68   1999
254'.8—dc21
          99-18660
          CIP

10   9   8   7   6   5   4   3   2   1

DEDICATION

Developing a Giving Church is dedicated to John C. Maxwell, a friend to Stan Toler and Elmer Towns on a journey of teaching stewardship to the Church of Jesus Christ.

John Maxwell has increased giving in every church that he has pastored, has taught stewardship through INJOY tapes and seminars, and has helped thousands of pastors teach stewardship to their churches. He also embodies stewardship through his personal discipleship to manage his time, talent, and treasure for the glory of God.

Thank you, John Maxwell, for your stewardship contribution to the Church of Jesus Christ.

Elmer Towns and Stan Toler

CONTENTS

Foreword   7

Acknowledgments   9

Introduction   11

1   *Developing a Giving Environment*   17

2   *Casting a Vision for a Giving Church*   41

3   *Developing Committed Steward Leaders*   69

4   *Developing an Annual Stewardship Plan*   91

5   *Supporting the Pastoral Team*   117

6   *Expanding the Giving Base*   139

Appendixes

    Stewardship Sermons   153

    Stewardship Stories   179

    Stewardship Quotes   191

    A Pastor's Stewardship Checklist   197

    Stewardship Bibliography   203

Notes   207

FOREWORD

This is a wonderful book by two of my best friends. Stan Toler began taking the stewardship journey with me at Faith Memorial Church, Lancaster, Ohio, where I began pastoring in 1973. Because we had been friends in college, I asked Stan to join the pastoral staff. In the first stewardship series in 1973, Stan preached a tremendous message, "The Stewardship of Time." I still remember that outstanding message because it focused on the congregation's total stewardship to God.

Elmer Towns is a mentor of mine who came to the Lancaster church in 1975 as the first speaker in my church growth conference. He did most of the speaking that year but encouraged me to be one of the main speakers in my conference. He told the pastors what God was doing in Faith Community Church.

The following year Towns came back and announced the Sunday morning text on Mal. 3:10, a well-known verse about tithing. "'Bring the whole tithe into the storehouse, that there may be food in my house. Test me in this,' says the LORD Almighty, 'and see if I will not throw open the floodgates of heaven and pour out so much blessing that you will not have room enough for it.'" I expected Towns to preach a sermon on money, but the sermon was on our stewardship to God. It was a sermon that developed one's faith. His emphasis that day was, "Prove Me Now." He challenged the people to demonstrate their faith to God by the way they gave money to God. The sermon had a profound influence on my church.

I love the thrust of this book: that stewardship is not fund-raising, nor is it a program developed to get more money from individuals. Stan Toler and Elmer Towns have developed the theme that stewardship is properly managing one's time, talent, and treasures for the glory of God.

I am thrilled that Stan and Elmer have joined forces together to produce this book, *Developing a Giving Church*. The strength of Stan's practical pastoral experience is seen in this book. Every church he has pastored has prospered financially. Elmer's strength is also seen in this book; he has researched the topics of stewardship to add an authoritarian credibility from the Word of God.

I pray that God will bless this book. May every pastor who has ever attended an INJOY conference read this book and build a strong giving church financially. And to pastors who have never been to an INJOY conference to hear Elmer or Stan, I encourage you to attend. I also recommend that you read this book to develop a strong program of stewardship. My prayer is that every person in your church will properly manage his or her time, talent, and treasures for the glory of God.

Sincerely yours,
John C. Maxwell
Founder, INJOY

ACKNOWLEDGMENTS

Special thanks . . .

To Michael Estep, Hardy Weathers, Kelly Gallagher, Bruce Nuffer, Shannon Hill, Paul Martin, and the entire Beacon Hill team. What a delight to work together with each one of you in ministry.

To Deloris Leonard, Derl Keefer, Pat Diamond, Norma Adams, Linda Williams, Renee Groms, and Jim Williams.

To Steve Weber, for encouraging us to write this book!

To Jerry Brecheisen, for creative insights, editorial assistance, and manuscript oversight.

INTRODUCTION

"Isn't it funny how $10 looks so big when we take it to church and so small when we take it to the store?" read a recent E-mail message. It's amusing considering the fact that $10 per week is the church attender's average donation.

In a Lilly endowed study of denominational funding, church finance author J. David Schmidt was asked what surprised him most about his research discoveries. He replied, "The biggest surprise was how little stewardship education is really going on in denominations today."

With similar results, a Christian Stewardship Association survey revealed that 85 percent of pastors feel they haven't been taught or empowered to teach principles of biblical stewardship and finance. It was also discovered that 90 percent of churches have no program to teach stewardship principles.

The *Leadership Network* calls it a "stealth crisis looming in the future." They add, "Few leaders are addressing the issue. It is an issue that affects every congregation, regardless of size or location, and every institution supported by organized religion." What is this "stealth crisis"? "It is the supply and distribution of money to support mission and ministry in the 21st century."

John and Sylvia Ronsvalle, in *Behind the Stained Glass Windows: Money Dynamic in the Church,* say, "Financial woes are the order of the day. Many smaller congregations are struggling to avoid having to close their doors. Many of the larger churches have had to scale back programs and put plans for expansion on indefinite hold. Older churches are saddled with historical landmarks—their buildings, which they are having trouble keeping in good repair, while newer churches are discovering the cost of having thrown up buildings too hastily a decade or two ago."[1]

Famed pollster George Gallup Jr. recently said, "One of the clear challenges facing churches and faith communities today is how to transform people into faithful, committed witnesses that are biblically rooted." He adds that there is a "grace that comes from giving, grace that is shared by both the donor and the beneficiary." Stephen Olford wrote, "Giving satisfies the soul, edifies the church, and magnifies the Lord." Obviously, the soul, the church, and the Lord get the "short straw" when Christians aren't trained to give.

There are over 2,300 references to money and possessions in the Word of God. At the same time prayer is only mentioned 500 times. Yet prayer is the very oxygen by which the soul breathes. The emphasis on giving is a reflection of our obedience to God's will revealed in our lives. It is a sign of Christian life. And those "vital signs" need to be checked now and then.

In a best-selling biography of John D. Rockefeller Sr., author Ron Chernow tells of Rockefeller's mother. Her hard work and her Christian faith held the family together in spite of the ungodly habits and frequent absences of their father. Her son, John, learned some important lessons both from his godly mother and from his ungodly father. His biographer suggests that as a result, he became a loving father who feared the effects that his riches might have on them. In fact, he was so concerned about teaching his children the wise use of material resources that he made them share a single bicycle.

Modern church leaders are heirs to greater wealth than Rockefeller's. They are heirs to the kingdom of heaven. Their Heavenly Father "owns the cattle on a thousand hills" and everything in those hills! Those leaders, then, must be aware of their responsibility to teach the wise use of God's resources. That "wise use" is called "stewardship."

Wise stewardship is seen in the giving habits of the congregation. Alarmingly, there has been a 26-year decline in giving percentages among Evangelicals, according to the CSA survey. And they further conclude that Christian giving has shrunk 1.5 to 3.5 percent, with "only 1 or 2 out of 10 Christians" giving 10 percent of their income to the Lord's work.

The story is told of a man who reported a horrible dream. "I dreamed that the Lord took my offering and multiplied it by ten, and this became my weekly income." He says, "Soon I lost my color TV, had to give up my new car, and I couldn't even make the payments on my new house." And then he added, "How can a fella live on $10 a week!"

A stewardship lesson certainly could have helped him deal with his nightmares. Yet, few pastors in the local church feel adequately equipped to teach stewardship principles. From a survey in *Leadership Journal*, David L. Goetz reported, "Almost two-thirds of pastors—63 percent—say their family practices a 10 percent, pretax tithe." And then he added an interesting survey result, "Oddly, while pastors tithe, they don't tell their congregations to. The study revealed that 35 percent of pastors don't preach what they practice."[2]

This book is an attempt to merge the principles of God's Word with proven methods for creating a climate for giving through stewardship education. It is also an attempt to equip those pastors to teach and preach God's principles for developing a giving church. It will help in six key ways:

1. It will provide vital information about stewardship in the local church.
2. It will be a resource of tested and tried stewardship materials.
3. It will help meet the needs of growing a church in financial matters.
4. It will educate church leaders in the area of stewardship.
5. It will provide a strategic plan of stewardship emphasis for the local church.
6. It will encourage those who do ministry to overcome frustration and stress through sound biblical teaching.

Maybe you've heard the story of the pastor who attempted a record-breaking missions offering by wiring the pews to an electrical current. He then asked the question, "How many will stand and pledge $100 to world missions?" The buzzer was pressed with "shocking results." Dozens immediately stood to their feet in an unprecedented response. However, it was also noted that several hesitant members were electrocuted!

Every church leader has met both groups somewhere in their leadership journey—those who get a "charge" out of giving and those who would rather die first. Our intent, in the pages that follow, is to help you minister to both.

- You will read some encouraging testimonies of how God turned rebellious hearts into joyful, giving hearts.
- You will hear from some well-known leaders who have discovered effective principles for developing a stewardship plan in the local church.
- You will read of some alarming local church giving trends. But you will also learn about some important methods that will help you reverse those trends in your church.
- You will learn how to avoid some financial pitfalls by applying some dynamic stewardship principles and plans.

John and Sylvia Ronsvalle, in their book *Behind the Stained Glass Windows: Money Dynamic in the Church*, warn, "The spiritual import of money has been largely ignored in churches. The silence of the church on the topic of money has meant that church members formed their attitudes toward their increasing resources as a result of consumer advertising and brought those attitudes back into the church."

This book is dedicated to God's chosen servants—servants who have seen the need to reverse the trends of secularism. It is dedicated to those who have a deep burden to reach the lost by every available means. And it is further dedicated to helping those servants find the means available for such a commission.

Stewardship is simply the wise management of God's resources. "The earth is the LORD's, and everything in it, the world, and all who live in it" (Ps. 24:1). A wise steward is called not only to faithfully manage those resources (see 1 Cor. 4:2) but also to teach others those management principles. *Developing a Giving Church* will help you do both.

Since stewardship is as much about living as it is about giving, many of the lessons that follow come from the classroom of our own experience. Others have been learned in the arena of common ministry with uncommon leaders who have been willing to share their dreams and designs as well as their disasters.

There's a story of a local church that wanted to build a new sanctuary. Among the few members—with even fewer dollars for such a project—was a successful contractor. The contractor agreed to build the church ABSOLUTELY FREE, if the church met two conditions. They would build the church as he saw fit, and they would not allow anyone to enter the building until the day it was dedicated.

After a glance at the checkbook, the board agreed to meet the conditions.

Construction was on schedule, but the church board was anxious for the day of the dedication service because they had not been allowed to see inside the building.

Dedication Sunday arrived, and the board thrilled to see their new facilities. But they were alarmed to see that there was only one row of pews in the sanctuary. They were also a bit curious about a control panel near the front of the church with their beloved contractor standing behind it.

Their curiosity turned to joy as the contractor pushed a button on the control panel and the row of pews slowly moved toward the front of the new sanctuary. "Wow!" they thought, "What an ingenious idea. Everyone will have the best view in the house!" The pastor was also thrilled. "No more back-seat-squatters that refuse to surrender their places to latecomers," he thought.

The preacher waxed eloquent in his dedicatory sermon. But the waxing and the eloquence lasted longer than the church board expected. They fidgeted and fussed as the minutes turned to an hour.

Suddenly, the contractor stood up and walked back to the control panel. And to the surprise of the church board, the contractor pushed another button. This time, the pulpit, along with the preacher still waxing eloquent, descended into the basement!

**"In response to the recent survey, I've decided to
stop harping on our serious financial needs."**

As you begin to practice and teach these principles for developing a giving church, a few of your parishioners will be looking for the "DOWN" button. Still, the great majority will want to move closer to the spiritual front as they see how God blesses their obedience in giving.

We pray that your speech will be seasoned with salt and that your heart will be filled with the spiritual "spoonful of sugar" that makes the medicine of truth go down easily. God's food is best served from one whose heart is filled with divine love. "Hope does not disappoint us, because God has poured out his love into our hearts by the Holy Spirit, whom he has given us" (Rom. 5:5).

Before World War II, there were children of Untouchables in a Christian school in India. Each year, at Christmas, they received presents from children in another Christian school in England. Each year the presents were the same—a doll for the girls and a toy for the boys.

On one occasion, the doctor from a nearby mission hospital was asked to distribute the gifts. During his visits, he told the children about a village far away where boys and girls had never heard of Jesus. He went on to suggest that some of them might even want to send their old dolls or toys to those children as presents. They liked the idea and planned for the doctor's return visit to collect the presents.

One week later, the doctor stood, as one by one, the children filed by to hand him a doll or a toy. To his surprise, they all handed him the new dolls and toys that had been distributed the previous week. When he asked them about it, a little girl spoke up, "Sir, when we thought about what God did for us by giving us His only Son, we decided that we couldn't give those boys and girls our old dolls and toys. He deserves our very best."

May God bless you as you give Him your best. And may God bless you as you teach others how to give their best. Your lives will be enriched as you surrender your *part* to God's glorious *wholeness*.

Elmer Towns and Stan Toler

DEVELOPING A GIVING ENVIRONMENT

Then your barns will be filled to overflowing, and your vats will brim over with new wine (Prov. 3:10).

><

"The most important aspect of tithing and stewardship is not the raising of money for the church, but the development of devoted Christians."
—Fred M. Wood

A YOUNG PREACHER HAD JUST FINISHED SEMINARY and had taken his first pastorate in the hills of Kentucky. Wanting to be effective in his preaching ministry, he walked into the pulpit on his first Sunday and preached on the evils of smoking. When he finished his message, some of the church leaders met him at the platform. "We're a little surprised that you would deal with the subject of smoking because nearly half of the state of Kentucky raises tobacco. You might want to think twice about talking about tobacco from this platform."

The preacher thanked them for enlightening him. The next Sunday he came back and preached against liquor and drinking. With great fervor, he preached on the ills of whiskey. The same group was standing near the platform after he finished. They said, "We think we need to tell you that you ought to be careful about preaching against alcoholic beverages, especially since nearly a third of our county distills whiskey."

"I didn't know that," the preacher replied. "Thank you for helping me." He came back the next Sunday to preach a stirring sermon on gambling—in any shape or form, the lotto, racehorses, or any other. The same group met him after the service. "We think we need to tell you that over half of our county raises thoroughbred racehorses, so you want to be real careful about talking about gambling from the pulpit."

Being a quick learner, the next Sunday, the young preacher preached against the evils of scuba diving in international waters!

Developing a giving environment has to do with learning— with developing new perspectives and new ideas based on the timeless truth of God's Word.

The Stewardship Attitude

John C. Maxwell talks about taking the "stew out of stewardship." Developing a giving church begins with the establishment of a biblical mind-set that takes the "stew" out of "stewardship." As usual, God is not silent regarding the matters of the heart and the lifestyle of His children. Notice this parable of Jesus:

> The kingdom of heaven is like a landowner who went out early in the morning to hire men to work in his vineyard. He agreed to pay them a denarius for the day and sent them into his vineyard.

> About the third hour he went out and saw others standing in the marketplace doing nothing. He told them, "You also go and work in my vineyard, and I will pay you whatever is right." So they went.

> He went out again about the sixth hour and the ninth hour and did the same thing. About the eleventh hour he went out and found still others standing around. He asked them, "Why have you been standing here all day long doing nothing?"

> "Because no one has hired us," they answered.

> He said to them, "You also go and work in my vineyard."

> When evening came, the owner of the vineyard said to his foreman, "Call the workers and pay them their wages, beginning with the last ones hired and going on to the first."

> The workers who were hired about the eleventh hour came and each received a denarius. So when those came who were hired first, they expected to receive more. But each one of them

also received a denarius. When they received it, they began to grumble against the landowner. "These men who were hired last worked only one hour," they said, "and you have made them equal to us who have borne the burden of the work and the heat of the day."

But he answered one of them, "Friend, I am not being unfair to you. Didn't you agree to work for a denarius? Take your pay and go. I want to give the man who was hired last the same as I gave you. Don't I have the right to do what I want with my own money? Or are you envious because I am generous."

So the last will be first, and the first will be last (*Matt. 20:1-16*).

In Jesus' parable about stewardship, God the Father is portrayed as the owner of all things, and in application, we are His managers. Stewards are *managers* of God's resources. Stewardship is not fund-raising. Stewardship is the management of time, talents, and resources for the glory of God.

Many churches emphasize stewardship to meet their budget needs. Actually the reverse is needed. The church should teach its people stewardship so they can be financially healthy, and when people are financially healthy, according to God's principles, they will give (tithe). Then the church will become healthy. In a local church, financially healthy families make for a financially healthy church.

People whose lives are relatively stable are more likely to donate to a church. Adults who experience relatively little change in their lives are considerably more likely to provide—and continue to provide—financial support to a church.

Rich Warren says that giving benefits his life in at least seven ways:

1. "Giving makes me more like God."
2. "Giving draws me closer to God."
3. "Giving breaks the grip of materialism."
4. "Giving strengthens my faith."
5. "Giving is an investment for eternity."
6. "Giving blesses me in return."
7. "Giving makes me happy."

In the parable of the laborers and the vineyard, there are five factors to consider:

▷ The owner—God

▷ The workers—us

▷ The work—our calling (v. 4)

▷ The pay—rewards for faithfulness and productivity

▷ The problem—the attitude people have toward their money—the workers in the parable had the same problem as most people in the world: they wanted more. "They expected to receive more" (v. 10).

Wrong Attitudes About Money

Wrong attitudes contribute to money problems in the church. Families are financially unhealthy because of their attitude toward money, not because of their circumstances. If the members of your congregation have the right attitude toward money—making money, saving money, and using money—they will get ahead in business, have strong families, and prosper in every part of their lives. The solution to money problems is not getting more money.

A little boy had two quarters, one for ice cream and one for the church offering. Unfortunately, he accidentally dropped one of the quarters into the storm sewer. "Well, Lord," the boy said, "there goes Your quarter!"

The solution is not about quarters. The solution to money problems is getting the right attitude toward money. A right attitude toward money will affect every other area of life.

Some people think that dropping 10 percent of their income into the offering plate is like rubbing a rabbit's foot—that God will do something magical in return. God is not a guaranteed lottery, where you buy a ticket and always win. When people pay their tithe to God, it is an evidence of a changed attitude, a renewed spirit. Tithers give to God out of gratitude, obedience, and worship.

Tithers give to God because of what He has given them. And, in the process of giving a tithe, their changed attitude produces other changes in their lives that will prosper them spiritually and financially.

People have wrong attitudes about money for several reasons. *First, they compare themselves with the "standard."* They feel "I deserve better." While it isn't wrong to desire better, and to work for better, it is wrong to demand better because of a selfish attitude and belligerent spirit.

Second, people have the wrong attitude about money because they compare themselves to others. For example, in an office situation, when one worker compares himself or herself to another person, a wrong attitude of jealousy and bitterness is usually the result. A spouse may declare, "You do more work than anyone in this house.

You deserve more." That may be a supportive opinion, but it's not necessarily the right one. In Jesus' parable of the laborers, some of them complained, "You have made them equal to us who have borne the burden of the work and the heat of the day" (v. 12). They were complaining that they had worked all day and had endured the hot sun, but those who had joined in the last hour got the same thing. In fact, if the owner had not come to the market and chosen them, they would have received nothing.

A third attitude is wrong perceptions and expectations. In the parable, the laborers "expected to receive more" (v. 10). Their expectations exceeded their actions. They wanted *more* for *less*. Like many modern workers, they wanted the benefits without putting in the hours.

Right Attitudes About Stewardship

Jesus' parable teaches us about right stewardship attitudes:

1. **We were useless until we were found in the marketplace.** Life is a marketplace of people waiting for the opportunity to do something. Every person has great potential waiting to be discovered. The laborers would have stayed in the marketplace all day if the owner had not come and given them a commission for service.

The owner's call (like God's call to us) was the beginning of their self-worth and their productivity. The workers had nothing to do until the owner issued them a call.

2. **The field belongs to the owner (God) and not to us.** The place where we work, whether in the church, in secular employment, or in any other place of ministry, is God's field. And He has sent us into the field. Jesus said, "I will build my church" (Matt. 16:18), and the possessive pronoun "my" indicates that the Church belongs to Him.

3. **The fruit (results) we harvest belongs to the owner (God) and not to us.** When we work for Jesus Christ, we must remember the fruit belongs to Jesus Christ. Too often we get possessive, and we think that the church (class, ministries, converts, etc.) belongs to us. He is the Lord of the harvest. It's not only His field but also His harvest. We are the workers. "Ask the Lord of the harvest, therefore, to send out workers into his harvest field" (Matt. 9:38).

4. **We are among many that serve the owner (God).** The field is not exclusively ours. Many are working with us in the field. The apostle Paul describes us as a part of a body, and as a part of the body we must always work in harmony; never in competition.

5. The owner judges us by our faithfulness and not by our fruit (success). What does the owner want from us? He wants a full day's work. He wants us to do our best. In one sense, with so many people working in the field, someone will probably work more productively than we will. The owner knows that not every worker will produce the same, so He judges each worker by his or her faithfulness. If a person will do the best that can be done with the tools he or she has, within the time allotted, the owner is satisfied with that effort.

6. The worst thing we can do is to be nonproductive. Workers were standing around the marketplace with nothing to do. When the owner of the field showed up, he asked the question, "Why have you been standing here all day long doing nothing?" (Matt. 20:6). God doesn't want His people to be idle while there is much to do in the field. Some think they can boycott God's work, sit down on the job, or even strike. But God would ask them, "Why have you been standing here all day long doing nothing?"

7. The owner (God) has total control over the field, the fruit, and the time of harvest. The owner has the right to make all of the choices because he is the owner. In the parable, the owner asks, "Don't I have the right to do what I want with my own money?" (v. 15). Obviously, the answer is yes. In our lives God can do with us what He pleases. It is our responsibility to yield to Him. He will guide us. And He will direct us.

8. The owner's plans (God's plans) for us are good. "I am generous" (v. 15), the owner reminded the workers. God wants us to prosper. "'For I know the plans I have for you,' declares the LORD, 'plans to prosper you and not to harm you'" (Jer. 29:11). Sometimes we take the initiative out of God's hand, because we do not trust Him. Our lack of faith in God's goodness causes us to mistrust His purpose. But His purpose is for us to prosper.

9. We must demonstrate our productivity by our faithfulness. It is not enough just to be put to work in the field. We must be faithful, and we must please the owner. It is not enough for someone to be called into ministry. They must go beyond that call and demonstrate that call in faithfulness, preparation, and service. In the parable, it was noted, "'Go and work in my vineyard, and I will pay you whatever is right.' So they went" (Matt. 20:4).

God Is the Ultimate Source

Developing a giving environment also includes a basic understanding about God's place in the finances of the church. He is the ultimate source of all things. "God is able to make all grace abound to you, so that in all things at all times, having all that you need, you will abound in every good work" (2 Cor. 9:8).

Every person is accountable to God because He gave us everything we have. God has given us our health, our bodies, our minds, our families, our material resources, our vocations, and our ministries. Stewardship includes the wise management of each of those areas.

Stewardship is illustrated with a triangle. God is the head of our universe. When we begin to teach biblical stewardship—the stewardship of life—there are several areas on which we need to focus: stewardship of relationships, stewardship of the gospel, stewardship of health, stewardship of wealth, and stewardship of gifts.

Samuel Bradburn was an associate of John Wesley. On one occasion Bradburn was in desperate financial need. When Wesley heard of his circumstances, he sent him a letter, "Dear Sammy: Trust in the Lord, and do good; so shalt thou dwell in the land, and verily thou shalt be fed. Yours affectionately, John Wesley." Wesley attached a 5-pound note (then worth about $10). Bradburn replied to his esteemed friend, "Rev. and Dear Sir: I have often been struck with the beauty of the passage of Scripture quoted in your letter, but I must confess that I never saw such a useful 'expository note' on it before."

Our giving is a great "expository note"—an explanation to others of our dependence upon God and His mercies. He is the source not only of our material possessions but also of our very lives. The apostle reminds us of that in the great sermon at Athens, "The God who made the world and everything in it is the Lord of heaven and earth and does not live in temples built by hands. And he is not served by human hands, as if he needed anything, because he himself gives all men life and breath and everything else" (Acts 17:24-25).

Stewardship Is an Act of Worship

Creating a giving environment includes acknowledging that God is the owner of all things, and all that is done should bring glory to Him. The great Nazarene evangelist Uncle "Buddie" Robinson used to say, "God owns the cattle on a thousand hills and all the 'taters' in those hills!" The act of giving is just another avenue for expressing love and gratitude to Him.

The stewardship-worship principle is seen in various Scripture settings as evidenced in the life of Jacob.

GOD

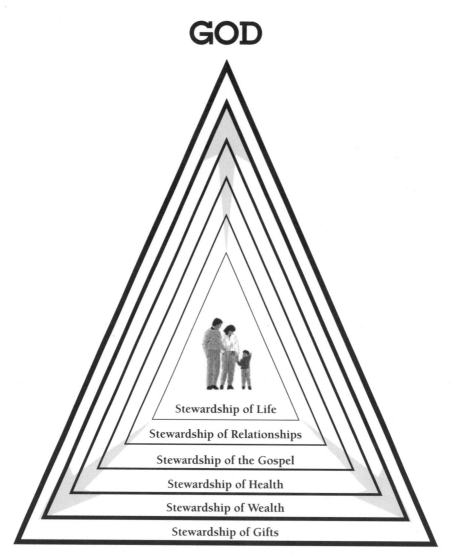

Source: Brian Kluth, Christian Stewardship Association. Adapted. Used by permission.

Jacob realized that all belongs to God, and he used his tithe as a means of worship.

When Jacob awoke from his sleep, he thought, "Surely the LORD is in this place, and I was not aware of it." He was afraid and said, "How awesome is this place! This is none other than the house of God; this is the gate of heaven."

Early the next morning Jacob took the stone he had placed

under his head and set it up as a pillar and poured oil on top of it. He called that place Bethel, though the city used to be called Luz.

Then Jacob made a vow, saying, "If God will be with me and will watch over me on this journey I am taking and will give me food to eat and clothes to wear so that I return safely to my father's house, then the LORD will be my God and this stone that I have set up as a pillar will be God's house, and of all that you give me I will give you a tenth" *(Gen. 28:16-22).*

Andrew Murray once said:

The world asks, "What does a man own?"

Christ asks, "How does he use it?"

The world thinks more about the money getting;

Christ, about the money giving.

And when a man gives, the world still asks, "What does he give?"

Christ asks, "How does he give?"

Author Waldo J. Werning adds another dimension. He says that God has given us a "trust account" and we need to acknowledge His deposits in that account by certain acts of stewardship "transfer":

Area	*Trust Account*	*Transfer*
1. Spiritual	salvation, faith, baptism, Communion, the Word, love	confess, witness, edify
2. Physical	body, time, food, strength	eat moderately, exercise, keep fit
3. Material	home, transportation, possessions, income, estate	Give God generous firstfruits, then prioritize spending on family and other areas
4. Abilities	knowledge, specific abilities, and spiritual gifts	Use in various ministries inside and outside the church
5. Relational	relatives, fellow Christians, Body of Christ	edify, fellowship, disciple, exhort, encourage[1]

Stewardship Supports the Local Church

Biblical stewardship is also God's method for supporting the local church. Notice the apostle Paul's advice to the Christians at Corinth:

> Remember this: Whoever sows sparingly will also reap sparingly, and whoever sows generously will also reap generously. Each man should give what he has decided in his heart to give, not reluctantly or under compulsion, for God loves a cheerful giver . . . As it is written: "He has scattered abroad his gifts to the poor: his righteousness endures forever." Now he who supplies seed to the sower and bread for food will also supply and increase your store of seed and will enlarge the harvest of your righteousness. You will be made rich in every way so that you can be generous on every occasion, and through us your generosity will result in thanksgiving to God. This service that you perform is not only supplying the needs of God's people but is also overflowing in many expressions of thanks to God (2 Cor. 9:6-7, 9-12).

Stephen Olford tells the story of a circus performer who earned a living by displaying astonishing feats of physical strength. His show normally concluded with an impressive demonstration of his ability to squeeze an orange dry. Everyone watched as he extracted a final drop of juice from the crushed orange. The performer always asked if someone in the audience would like to try to squeeze another drop out of the rind that he had already squeezed dry.

One day, a rather frail audience member said, "I'll do it." The little guy stepped onto the stage and took the orange rind from the circus strongman. The spectators laughed as the man held up the shriveled piece of rind. The atmosphere was electric, and after a moment or two, to everyone's amazement, a drop of orange juice dropped to the floor as the man squeezed the rind. The audience cheered.

When the cheers subsided, the circus strongman asked the little man to explain how he had developed such amazing powers. "Nothing to it," the man replied with a grin, "I happen to be the treasurer of my church."

Many church treasurers are expected to have just that kind of power. They're expected to take care of all the money problems in the church. What church treasurer hasn't been concerned, when sitting down to distribute moneys for the monthly bills, that there seemed to be more *month* than *money?*

Imagine what a difference it might make if most of your parishioners believed that God expects each of them to fund the church generously. Such funding of the church is exemplified in Early Church times:

> Those who accepted his message were baptized, and about three thousand were added to their number that day.
>
> They devoted themselves to the apostles' teaching and to the fellowship, to the breaking of bread and to prayer. Everyone was filled with awe, and many wonders and miraculous signs were done by the apostles. All the believers were together and had everything in common. Selling their possessions and goods, they gave to anyone as he had need (*Acts 2:41-45*).

The generosity of the Early Church is of particular interest. Those who had possessions, land, and durable goods sold them and put the proceeds into a common treasury. Expenditures were paid out of the treasury.

William M. Easum says the church must shift from "thinking about raising money to developing disciples." He adds, "Our problem is spiritual, and until we approach it as a spiritual issue, we will get nowhere. God does not honor money raising. God honors servant discipleship. To deal with our financial problems, we must return to our first love of making disciples of Jesus Christ."

Money Is a Sensitive Subject

Recently, two morning radio talk-show hosts were discussing a famous athlete's signing bonus. The one noted that the athlete called himself a Christian and told the press that the "Lord had instructed him to sign the contract." The other DJ responded that the Lord probably told him to sign it so that 10 percent would go to the church. His partner retorted, "You know, I've always been suspicious as to where that money really goes!"

The church is not a stranger to that suspicion. Money is a sensitive subject, and people have a tendency to be protective of their resources, and to be quite defensive when questioned about them. They may ask, "Where does that money go? And what right does the church have to concern itself with *my* money?" However, the Scripture says with inescapable clarity that the Lord is honored through our possessions, regardless of how vast or meager, "Honor the LORD with your wealth, with the firstfruits of all your crops; then your barns will be filled to overflowing, and your vats will brim over with new wine" (Prov. 3:9-10).

You've heard the expression "money talks." Often the "conversation" is disturbing. G. Stuart Briscoe, in his book *Choices for a Lifetime*,[2] tells about the responses of ordinary Americans to a question posed by researchers working on a book titled *The Day America Told the Truth*. The question? What would you do for $10 million? Twenty-five percent of those who responded said they would leave their families! The same number would leave their churches and/or religion, and 23 percent said they would be a prostitute for a week or more. Seven percent of those responding were willing to kill a stranger!

After the survey was taken, the researchers wondered if the $10 million tab had been too tempting; so they asked the same people what they would do for $5 million, for $4 million, or for $3 million. The responses were the same. The good news is that at $2 million, people began to have second thoughts.

Money Problems in the Church

The church faces several significant challenges that affect its giving environment and often restrict its outreach to the community. **The first challenge is the need to attract younger givers.** A large number of people born after 1946 do not understand the importance of giving to the local church.

Someone commented, "People no longer give to the church simply because it is the church. The church must prove it is worthy of donations through the mark it leaves on the world."

Inquiring minds just want to know . . .
- How is the church spending its dollars?
- Who is being impacted by their gifts?
- Will souls be reached for Christ?

In a day of demands for customer satisfaction, and loads of options for the consumer, there should be integrity in all dealings. The focus must be on the proper management of church dollars.

Someone has aptly stated that the old wisdom about giving was, "We don't have to persuade people to support the church; that's God's job." The new wisdom is, "We must effectively convey to our people what we stand for, how we minister, and what difference it makes in people's lives."

Obviously, the church leadership must take a good look at its stewardship emphasis. But is there any new word about stewardship? Probably not. What needs to be done, however, is to recast the basics—return to consistent and faithful teaching of the Word of God in its emphasis on the stewardship of life and giving as the Lord has prospered.

The church needs to hear again that stewardship is more than money. C. Neil Strait recently said, "The church that feels its stewardship base is covered when it has raised money and completed its pledge campaign is neglectful and wanting in its teaching."

Second, there is the challenge of accountability. The abuses by a storied few have made a tremendous impact upon the lives of many. Each new revelation, noted carefully by the media, makes the public question the money practices of the church. Because of that credibility crisis, there are three questions that must be answered by church leaders:

1. *"Is financial information available to the church members?"* People in our churches need to have the assurance that everything is aboveboard and open.

There should be no secrets, so one statement that needs to be made to a congregation constantly is, "Our books are always open for your perusal. If you need to see something, you can." However, it must be clarified that individual giving records are personal and private, so they are not available. Seldom will people ask to see the books, but they must have the opportunity, and they must have the assurance that the church is taking good care of their dollars.

Carl Bangs writes, "There should be no secrecy at any level. Sensitive matters may be withheld from the general public on occasion, but they should not be hidden from those who are responsible for oversight and review."[3]

2. *"Are moneys cared for properly?"* Is there a proper counting system? Is there more than one counter? As you develop a giving environment, your people will want to be "in the know" about financial matters. They will want to know whether your church can be trusted with their finances. Carl Bangs adds further, "In dealing with the Lord's money, it is as spiritual to attend to the auditor's report as it is to hear the report on evangelism and church growth."

In Jesus' parable of the talents, the owner gave talents to each of his servants. The servants were to use their talents while their master was gone on his journey. They didn't know when he would return. Matthew records, "After a long time the master of those servants returned and settled accounts with them" (Matt. 25:19). On a final day, all of the accounts will be "settled." Every believer will be subject to the divine audit where everything that is hidden will be revealed.

In the meantime, Christ calls His Church to careful consideration that every action, or transaction, is carried out to the glory of God and the edifying of the church.

3. *"Is restraint used when borrowing money for buildings and outreach endeavors?"* The authors could cite several incidents that have occurred over the last 25 years in local churches that are almost criminal as it relates to church debt. Ponder Gilliland was so right when he said that if we worked on the principle of thirds, we'd never get into trouble. Gilliland preached an ideal formula of: One-third for personnel, one-third for program or ministry, and one-third for property. While the "ideal" is not always achievable, that kind of balance will help keep churches from financial problems and will also bring a great deal of credibility.

Another stewardship challenge involves **pastoral changes**. For instance, in some denominations, the pastor serves less than three years in a local church. It's almost as if the pastor's furnished vehicle ought to be a U-haul truck! With short tenure, developing any type of continuity is very difficult, as far as stewardship goes, in the local congregation.

Some church leaders have suggested that a pastor doesn't even make a significant impact on a community in less than five years. Certainly, the pastor who has been established in an area over many years has greater credibility, and that pastor's church has greater credibility. People want to know what the leader expects of them and, in turn, whether the leader will be committed as well.

A church was having a problem meeting its budget. The pastor suggested to the board that a special fund be established to meet the crisis. During the discussion, the pastor recommended that the leaders set an example by being the first to contribute to the emergency budget fund.

As he made the suggestion, he looked straight into the eyes of a board member who was "well-to-do." The problem was, the board member was known not only to be a man of means but also to be one of the community's stingiest men. Feeling the obligation of the pastor's call to make a financial commitment, the board member finally spoke up, "Preacher, I'll give $25."

Just then, a small piece of plaster fell from the ceiling and hit the board member on the head. "I'll make that $50!" he quickly declared. The church treasurer was heard to pray, "Hit 'im again, Lord, hit 'im again!"

A pastor who is known to be a continual positive influence in the community will affect those who are looking for a church home.

A fourth challenge is the eroding base of regular givers. This is especially a problem as we enter the 21st century and the number of givers in the congregation decreases. Biblical stewardship training must be a priority.

For example, the average senior in your church gives seven times more than the average baby boomer, or baby buster for that matter. Barna research reported the percentage of givers per age group: "31 percent of Baby Busters (18-32 years old), 43 percent of Baby Boomers (33-51 years old), 54 percent of Builders (52-69 years old), 61 percent of Seniors (70 or older).[4] In the same research data, it was concluded that "a person's greatest earning years come in their 50s and early 60s." The greatest givers are usually the more mature members in the church. Pastor Mark Toler-Hollingsworth, during Stewardship Month at his church in Edmond, Oklahoma, told his members, "God help us if our seniors die off suddenly! We would go broke if something happened to them." So, we've got to find a way to expand the giving base of local churches. The fact is, a church can never grow beyond the dimensions of its base, or its ability to care for people. Without an expanded giving base, the church faces difficult times in the days ahead.

Churchman and pollster Russ Bredholt says there are predictors of giving. Some of those predictors include:
- Income
- Education
- Church involvement
- Personal faith
- Size of the congregation
- Age
- Children in the family
- Stewardship materials
- Attitudes about the church and/or pastor

Notice the predictor of church involvement, for instance. One way to increase a people's giving is to get them involved in the ministries of the local church. Russ Bredholt has often said that you can use involvement as a gauge for giving. Involvement influences giving. Dean Hoge, author of *National Contextual Factors Influencing Church Trends,* says, "Regularity of church attendance remains the number one predictor of an individual's contributions to the church."[5]

Some would say, "Well, that's not the seeker-sensitive model, that's not a 'Willow Creek' model." They may add, "You don't have to say anything, you don't have to sign anything, you don't have to sing anything, you don't have to give anything in a seeker-sensitive church."

In fact, Bill Hybels, Willow Creek's dynamic pastor, remarked at an INJOY conference recently, "In the early days of our church we had a lot of baby Christians running around who didn't have a clue about stewardship, so each year I preach a full series on biblical stewardship. This year's series is on 'Achieving Financial Freedom.'"

Many have attended a Bill Hybels conference and have decided, "We won't receive offerings anymore in our church. We'll just put a box out back and hope for the best." But in a recent Willow Creek conference of over 20,000 people, Hybels said, "We have too many squatters on the East side of Jordan, we have too many gold-brickers here. We've got to have some folks who are going to dig in and help us." That's saying to the saints, "Get with the program," and that is exactly what must be done if the giving base in your church is to be expanded.

The fifth challenge is affluence. Prosperity, health, and wealth preaching has cost the church a great deal. Famous PTL leader and former health-wealth-and-prosperity preacher Jim Bakker states in his book *I Was Wrong,* "When it comes to the health, wealth, and prosperity message, I was wrong."[6] Some preachers try to convince their audience that if they would give *"to get,"* they would have a wonderful life. In recent months, Mr. Bakker has opted for a simpler life of ministry in the inner city of a major metropolitan area. Gone are the days of penthouse suites and luxury cars.

Chuck Millhuff says, "You give to get, *to give again."* That's truly "Giving Living." A country song said it so well, "Nobody wants to play rhythm guitar behind Jesus; / Everybody wants to be the lead singer in the band." That's part of the problem in the local church. Some folks give only if they can gain control—they give if they can sing a solo, give if they can be out front, they give if their name is in the bulletin or on the signboard. That has to change, because when we talk about the stewardship of life, we talk about a people who are God-centered, not me-centered.

The sixth challenge is vision casting. Dave Sutherland says it right when he says, "People tend to give to what captures their imagination." A recent lottery drawing promised nearly one quarter of a billion dollars. Reporters stopped along the winding trail of "millionaire wannabes" waiting outside convenience stores. "What will you do with the money?" they asked. The answers were as varied as personalities of those standing in line. Most of them began to project on the wonderful deeds they would do for their families and their communities. Several gave a unique North American view of classic greed. All of them had a wonderful sense of expectancy, however. Their imaginations had been captured by "Powerball promises." What captures the imagination of your congregation?

"Givers needed, apply within!"
—A Church Sign, Welch, West Virginia

The final challenge is in the **development of steward leaders who model giving.** The first source of giving models is the Bible. Great leaders, mentioned in the Bible, offer insights and illustrations to help you create a giving environment in the local church. For example, there is the story of King David in the midst of a building program. Moses is another example of one who led people through a building project. The prophet Nehemiah led God's people through a major renovation program. The apostle Paul established a relief-fund ministry.

As you teach from the lives and ministries of these great Bible characters, you offer your congregation biblical models for their giving.

Stewardship Decisions

David Livingstone wrote in his journal on one occasion:
>   People talk of the sacrifice I have made in spending so much of my life in Africa. Can that be called a sacrifice which is simply paying back a small part of the great debt owing to our God, which we can never repay? Is that a sacrifice which brings its own blest reward in healthful activity, the consciousness of doing good, peace of mind and a bright hope of a glorious destiny hereafter? Away with the word in such a view and with such a thought! It is emphatically no sacrifice. Say rather it is a privilege.

How insightful! Livingstone thankfully responded to the call of Rom. 12:1-2: "Therefore, I urge you, brothers, in view of God's

MODEL	NEED	METHODS	REFERENCES
King David	Building Project	■ Planning Time Alone with God ■ Large Lead Gift Given ■ Leadership Meeting and Gifts ■ Gifts-in-Kind	□ 1 Chron. 28:12, 19 □ 1 Chron. 29:2-5 □ 1 Chron. 29:5-9 □ 1 Chron. 29:8
Moses	Building Project	■ Large Group Meeting ■ Offerings Accepted ■ Skilled Volunteer Labor	□ Exod. 35:4 □ Exod. 20:34; 36:3-7 □ Exod. 35:10, 30-35
Nehemiah	Building Renovations Annual Funding	■ Personal Prayer ■ Major Donor Call ■ Government Grant ■ Executive Planning ■ Pivotal Leadership Meeting ■ Volunteer Labor ■ Debt Counseling and Action ■ Executive Salaries Reduced ■ Personal Lead Gift ■ Leadership Gifts ■ Public Gifts ■ Signed Stewardship Covenant ■ Development Office Established ■ Reorganization Plan	□ Neh. 1:4-11 □ Neh. 2:1-8 □ Neh. 2:7-8 □ Neh. 2:11-16 □ Neh. 2:17-18 □ Neh. 3; 4:14-21; 6:15 □ Neh. 5:1-13 □ Neh. 5:14-15, 18 □ Neh. 7:70 □ Neh. 7:70-71 □ Neh. 7:72 □ Neh. 9:37; 10:39 □ Neh. 12:44-47 □ Neh. 13:4-14
King Joash	Building Renovations	■ Development Staff Failure ■ Designated Giving Program	□ 2 Kings 12:4-8 □ 2 Kings 12:9-16
King Hezekiah	Annual Funding	■ Personal Gift ■ Leadership Announcement ■ Development Department Established	□ 2 Chron. 31:3 □ 2 Chron. 31:4-10 □ 2 Chron. 31:11-21
King Solomon	Annual Funding	■ Major Donor Relations	□ 1 Kings 10:1-10 □ 1 Kings 4:7, 27, 28
Ezra	Building Renovations	■ Major Donor Relations ■ Freewill Offerings ■ Government Grant ■ Leadership Gifts	□ Ezra 7:6, 15 □ Ezra 7:16 □ Ezra 6:3-15; 7:11-23 □ Ezra 2:68-69
Apostles	Benevolence Ministry	■ Foundation Board ■ Personal Donor Relations	□ Acts 4:34; 5:2 □ Acts 5:3-11
Jesus	General Fund	■ Personal Ministry Relations ■ Stretching Provided Resources	□ Luke 8:2-3 □ Matt. 14:17-21
Paul	Relief Ministry	■ Large Group Mailing ■ Stewardship Teaching ■ Field Representatives	□ 1 Cor. 16:1-3 □ 2 Cor. 8—9 □ 2 Cor. 8:16-24
Elijah	General Fund	■ Miraculous Provision ■ One-on-One Donor Calls ■ Stewardship Teaching	□ 1 Kings 17:1-7 □ 1 Kings 17:8-16 □ 1 Kings 17:13-14
Joshua	Relocation Project	■ Strategic Marketing and Expansion Plan	□ Josh. 24
Haggai	Ministry and Building Needs	■ Stewardship Teaching	□ Haggai 1

Source: Brian Kluth
Christian Stewardship Association
Web site: www.stewardship.org

mercy, to offer your bodies as living sacrifices, holy and pleasing to God—this is your spiritual worship. Do not conform any longer to the pattern of this world, but be transformed by the renewing of your mind. Then you will be able to test and approve what God's will is—his good, pleasing and perfect will."

Good stewardship decisions are made with God's Word in view. The psalmist advises, "The statutes of the LORD are trustworthy, making wise the simple" (Ps. 19:7). God will never lead you, nor will He lead your church, contrary to His revealed Word.

There is no stewardship manual on earth that should be substituted for the Bible. What God has to say is infinitely greater than what any earthly adviser has to say. Spend time in His Word before you design your stewardship plans for the local church.

"Trust the guidance of the Word and the gentle nudging of the Holy Spirit."
—Jerald Johnson

In his last years of service in Africa, when Livingstone was running out of time and his strength was low, he revealed the true motivation for his undaunted, selfless service in his tribute to his Lord and Savior, Jesus Christ. He wrote: "He is the greatest master I have ever known. If there is any one greater, I do not know him. Jesus Christ is the only master worth serving. He is the only ideal that never loses its inspiration. He is the only friend whose friendship meets every demand. He is the only Savior who saves us to the uttermost. We go forth in His name, in His power, and in His Spirit to serve Him."

Build your plans on a solid foundation. The Word of God reminds us: "Each one should be careful how he builds. For no one can lay any foundation other than the one already laid, which is Jesus Christ. If any man builds on this foundation using gold, silver, costly stones, wood, hay or straw, his work will be shown for what it is, because the Day will bring it to light. It will be revealed with fire, and the fire will test the quality of each man's work"(1 Cor. 3:10-13).

"It was in the teachings of the Apostle Paul that Christian stewardship formed a major place in biblical tradition."

—T. K. Thompson

Peter said, "These have come so that your faith—of greater worth than gold, which perishes even though refined by fire—may be proved genuine and may result in praise, glory and honor when Jesus Christ is revealed" (1 Pet. 1:7). God's approval is worth infinitely more than human applause. If it's a choice between great buildings and God's blessing, choose God's blessing.

Souls Must Be Our First Priority

Jesus gave us a very important caution in His parable of the rich fool.

> The ground of a certain rich man produced a good crop. He thought to himself, "What shall I do? I have no place to store my crops." Then he said, "This is what I'll do. I will tear down my barns and build bigger ones, and there I will store all my grain and my goods. And I'll say to myself, 'You have plenty of good things laid up for many years. Take life easy; eat, drink and be merry.'"
>
> But God said to him, "You fool! This very night your life will be demanded from you. Then who will get what you have prepared for yourself?"
>
> This is how it will be with anyone who stores up things for himself but is not rich toward God (*Luke 12:16-21*).

Church leaders must never lose sight of the mission of Jesus, which was "to seek and to save what was lost." Church ministry is not about raising buildings. It's about reaching souls. Plans and properties and personnel are simply tools used for the more important work—reaching lost souls.

Better barns and greater storehouse inventories are meaningless if it means a spiritual distance between people and God. Every effort must be made to bring our energies to the "first concern" of the church.

God's Math Takes Care of Our Fears

"The disciples came to Jesus in private and asked, 'Why couldn't we drive it out?' He replied, 'Because you have so little faith. I tell you the truth, if you have faith as small as a mustard seed, you can say to this mountain, "Move from here to there" and it will move. Nothing will be impossible for you'" (Matt. 17:19-20).

A little boy was chastised by his mother for taking the largest piece of pie at the dinner table. "Son, why did you take the largest piece of pie and leave the smaller pieces for our company?" she asked.

"I'm sorry, Mom," her son replied. "Which piece would you have taken?"

"I would have taken the smallest piece," she answered.

"Well, Mom," the little boy said with a smile that covered his face, "it's still there!"

Often, our lack of faith causes us to choose the smallest pieces. The writer to the Hebrews teaches us, "Faith is being sure of what we hope for and certain of what we do not see" (11:1).

Jesus taught that it doesn't take big faith to see big results. The disciples weren't chided for the *size* of their faith; they were chided because of the *source* of their faith. Faith in human resources brings minimal results. Faith in God's resources brings mountainous results!

><><

"There is always time to do what is right."
—Martin Luther King Jr.

Christian Benevolence Must Not Be Secondary

As has already been established, stewardship is management. Dr. Steve Weber often says, "Developing a giving environment will demand a Sprit-led and mercy-filled management of the time, talent, and treasure of your church members." Paul charged Timothy with another "great" commission.

"In the presence of God and of Christ Jesus, who will judge the living and the dead, and in view of his appearing and his kingdom, I give you this charge: Preach the Word; be prepared in season and out of season; correct, rebuke and encourage—with great patience and careful instruction" (2 Tim. 4:1-2).

Notice several important factors in that commission. (1) He was obedient to God. He wasn't to be a lord over those who worked with him. Timothy was to be mindful that whatever he asked of others, he would have to be willing to do himself. (2) He preached God's Word. He couldn't expect to teach others something he had not experienced firsthand. Brian Kluth says, "When you teach from the head it goes to the head, but when you teach from a life it goes to a life." The Word of God was to be evident in his life as well as in his work. (3) He cared for the needs of his ministry team members. Successful ministry leaders are sensitive to the unique emotional, spiritual, and relational needs of each worker. The biblical quality of mercy was to be evident in his leadership.

〜〜

"We make a living by what we get; we make a life by what we give."
—Winston Churchill

Focus on the Family

Again, Paul gave some valuable advice to Timothy, "If anyone does not know how to manage his own family, how can he take care of God's church?" (1 Tim. 3:5). Each church leader probably knows of someone who suffered by living in the shadow of a "famous" parent. In seeking ministry successes, remember that success begins at home—managing the time, talent, and treasures of the family God has given you. It's better to be known for your attention to your family than to be well-known for your professional achievements.

Focus on Spirit-Producing Life Ministries

Church development promotions have run the gamut from preaching on rooftops to swallowing goldfish. One church special-ordered 200 goldfish from a church bus ministry magazine. To the horror of the pastor and Sunday School superintendent, the order didn't arrive until the Saturday afternoon before the Sunday morning event. And adding to the horror, the "sale" fish were all "DOA!" The Sunday School superintendent got rid of as many as he could by explaining that the lifeless little "fishes" were doing the backstroke!

Gimmicks and inventive promotions are acceptable if they are not substitutes for Bible-centered teaching and God-honoring outreach. Substance counts most. A donor expansion program must be based on rock-solid principles. "Seek first his kingdom and his righteousness, and all these things will be given to you as well" (Matt. 6:33).

"A great deal of our ineffectiveness can be attributed to ignoring the Holy Spirit."
—Oswald Sanders

There once was a farmer who was well-known for his generosity. His friends could not understand how he could give so *much* and yet remain able to give even *more*. "We cannot understand how you *do* it," they said. "You give far *more* than any of the rest of us, and yet you always seem to have more to *give*." To which the farmer replied, "Oh, that is *easy* to explain. You see, I keep shoveling into *God's* bin, and God keeps shoveling back into *mine*—and God has the *bigger* shovel."

It is incredibly easy to get caught up in "the chase" and forget the purpose of a stewardship campaign. It is not about meeting goals. It is not about raising money. It is not about beating last year's totals or out-*raising* other churches. A stewardship campaign is about ministering to your people so they can minister to others. It's about giving your people the opportunity of joyful obedience and servanthood.

"Give, and it will be given to you. A good measure, pressed down, shaken together and running over, will be poured into your lap. For with the measure you use, it will be measured to you."
—Luke 6:38

2 CASTING A VISION FOR A GIVING CHURCH

"Bring the whole tithe into the storehouse, that there may be food in my house. Test me in this," says the LORD Almighty, "and see if I will not throw open the floodgates of heaven and pour out so much blessing that you will not have room enough for it" (Mal. 3:10).

><><

"There never was a person who did anything worth doing who did not receive more than he gave."
—Henry Ward Beecher

A COLORFUL EASTERN OHIO PREACHER ONCE SAID that God promised He would open the windows of heaven for those who tithe. "What about 5 percent?" someone asked. "No!" the preacher replied, "God doesn't do windows for less than 10 percent!"

Casting a vision for a giving church begins with the clear-cut teaching of biblical stewardship principles in preaching, worship, and publication ministries. The Ten Commandments have never been influenced by inflation, neither has the principle of the tithe—the tenth.

Robert A. Laidlaw, the New Zealand businessman and famous author, started tithing at age 18. His salary was $3 a week. Later he promised God he would give 10 percent and would continually increase the amount as his income increased. At 25 years of age, Laidlaw increased his tithing to 50 percent! That's right! He gave 50 percent of all his earnings back to God. Nearly 50 years later he reflected, "In spiritual communion and in material things, God has blessed me a hundredfold, and has graciously entrusted to me a stewardship far beyond my expectations when, as a lad of 18, I started to give God a definite portion of my wages."

Sir John Templeton, chairman of the $15 billion Templeton fund is quoted in a *Christian Stewardship Association* publication, "I have watched over 100,000 families over my years of investment counseling. I always saw greater prosperity and happiness among those families who tithed than among those who didn't."[1]

Robert Wuthrow, author of *The Crisis in the Churches: Spiritual Malaise, Fiscal Woe,* says, "Of every $1,000 received by churches, $900 comes from people who work in middle-class occupations. Those who believe it is important to give a percentage of their income to God give about $1,000 more per year."[2]

"The measure of our giving must be the measure of God's giving."

—Paul Cunningham

In the Beginning, Giving

The act of giving the substance of our life to God goes back to the beginning of Scripture. From the outset, giving money involved itself with the act of salvation and worship.

"Cain brought some of the fruits of the soil as an offering to the LORD. But Abel brought fat portions from some of the firstborn of his flock. The LORD looked with favor on Abel and his offering, but on Cain and his offering he did not look with favor. So Cain was very angry, and his face was downcast" (Gen. 4:3-5).

God's principles for giving are clearly seen even in that first act of giving. First, "Abel offered God a better sacrifice than Cain did" (Heb. 11:4). The giving of gifts was linked to his faith in God. Second, God wasn't pleased with all of the gifts. The gifts had to follow the pattern He gave. Third, giving must be accompanied by a right attitude.

> "None of these temporal things are yours; you are only stewards of them, not proprietors. God is the Proprietor of all: He lodges them in your hands for a season; but they are still His property. Rich men, understand and consider this. If your steward uses any part of your estate (so called in the language of men) any further or any otherwise than you direct, he is a knave: he has neither conscience nor honour. Neither have you one or the other, if you use any part of that estate which is in truth God's not yours, any otherwise than He directs."
>
> —John Wesley's translation of Luke 16:12

Notice these principles for Christian giving as revealed in Scripture:

1. God deserves my best. "Honor the LORD with your wealth, with the firstfruits of all your crops" (Prov. 3:9).

Some years ago, while he was president of Eastern Nazarene College, Edward S. Mann told Samuel Young about a generous gift of $25,000 from the Kresge Foundation to the Development Fund of Eastern Nazarene College. Stanley S. Kresge, vice-chairman of the board of the S. S. Kresge Company, delivered the check and underscored the true meaning of their gift by the inscription, *In the name and for the sake of Jesus Christ.* Samuel Young was quoted as saying, "Surely this motivation is adequate for all of us and challenges us to *plus giving* in every area of our lives!"

2. God will get my best each week. "On the first day of every week, each one of you should set aside a sum of money [for the offering]" (1 Cor. 16:2a).

3. God will get a minimum of 10 percent as each person gives "in keeping with his income" (1 Cor. 16:2b).

"The tithe is a wonderful goal but a terrible place to stop."

—Bill Hybels

4. God will be glorified through my gifts, "always giving thanks to God the Father for everything in the name of our Lord Jesus Christ" (Eph. 5:20).

Waldo J. Werning asks, "What moves men as stewards?" He writes, "Think of the many options available for perverting man's true motive for stewardship; the general good of the Kingdom, group pressure, pride or embarrassment, social approval, pity, tax exemption, conscience salving, fear, owing the tithe, humanitarian ideas, loyalty, example of Christ, rewards, and pursuit of happiness."[3]

Werning suggests that the enduring solution he sees is "to teach the gospel so that the Holy Spirit knocks down human barriers in the heart and builds a house of love in the same place." He goes on to say, "God is concerned about motives: 'Be not deceived; God is not mocked: for whatsoever a man soweth, that shall he also reap. For he that soweth to his flesh shall of the flesh reap corruption; but he that soweth to the Spirit shall of the Spirit reap life everlasting' (Gal. 6:7-8)."[4]

5. God will be praised through my gifts. "Each man should give what he has decided in his heart to give, not reluctantly or under compulsion, for God loves a cheerful giver" (2 Cor. 9:7).

> **"Stewardship always starts with a repentant heart, a change of mind concerning our opinion about earthly values."**
>
> **—John A. Knight**

The outstanding characters of the Bible were givers. They regularly, proportionately, cheerfully, and thankfully brought their offerings to God. For example, Noah built an altar and gave an offering to the Lord after his departure from the ark (Gen. 8:20). Following the promise of God to Abraham that he would receive the land of Canaan, Abraham made an offering (12:7).

The offerings in those days were quite simple. There was no temple to maintain, there were no priests in need of a salary. The gift was usually a lamb that was slain and consumed in the act of sacrifice.

The Principle of the Tithe

The divine standard for stewardship is faithfulness, and God identifies indifference and slothfulness along with wickedness (Matt. 25:26). *Slothfulness* is a bad word in Jesus' vocabulary and can even control destinies (vv. 34-46).

Christian stewardship also reaches to our deepest treasures and resources. It involves our money or net income. The gospel is not "inside stuff"; it is something to be shared. Even Emerson observed, "Your goodness must have some edge to it, else it is none." One of the "edges" available in our day is the matter of giving. It is the challenge of New Testament Christians—even in the 21st century—to pay tithes of our salaries, or wages, or net income to the building and extension of God's kingdom through the church of our alignment.

Actually, the tithe is not a ceiling; it is a floor. We are inclined to identify giving basically as a grace. This involves God's enabling. John Wesley used to observe frequently, "The commands of God are only covered promises."

"Tithing" means a believer gives one-tenth of his or her income to the Lord. "Storehouse tithing" means that the tithe is given to the local church. It is God's "commonsense way of growth." Everyone gives according to his or her ability, and together, enough money is raised to carry on the ministry of preaching the gospel.

The first occurrence of tithing came when Abraham met Melchizedek, the first mentioned priest of God. As Abraham returned from the victory over Chedorlaomer, he was met by Melchizedek, the King of Salem. In the Book of Hebrews, Melchizedek is a type of the priesthood of Jesus Christ. Since the priest had a ministry to individuals, Melchizedek gave Abraham bread and wine. In return for this ministry, Abraham "gave him a tenth of everything" (Gen. 14:20).

Interestingly, when the first priest of God appears in the Bible, tithes are collected to support him. Also, tithes were paid at a *place* that later would be connected with tithes. Melchizedek was king of "Salem," a place we know today as Jerusalem.

The next occurrence of tithing comes when Jacob is at Bethel, also a place later approved for religious worship. There, Jacob saw a symbol of salvation, the ladder reaching to heaven. Jacob, knowing that the presence of God was there, named the place "Bethel," the house of God. He vowed that if God would bless him, he would return: "This stone that I have set up as a pillar will be God's house, and of all that you give me I will give you a tenth" (Gen. 28:22).

Before the Israelites left Egypt, they were first instructed to "borrow" gold, silver, and jewels from their Egyptian neighbors (Exod. 11:1-2). Second, they were to make preparation for celebrating the first Passover. The borrowing of jewels and raiment by the Israelites became the seed-plot for God's people to make gifts: (1) to build the Tabernacle, (2) to sustain the ministry of the Tabernacle, and (3) to support the priesthood.

There is an interesting teaching principle in the account. God never asks for contributions but what He first supplies resources.

God chose an unusual way to make sure the Israelites would have gifts to contribute toward the construction of the Tabernacle and its furnishings by allowing them to "spoil the Egyptians." He can use routine or special ways to make sure we have something to give toward His work. It's always amazing to see how God provides resources to use in His work!

The new
"Insta-Tithe" made
giving a snap!

Tithing in the New Testament

Jesus underscored the importance of the tithe in His word to the Pharisees, "Woe to you, teachers of the law and Pharisees, you hypocrites! You give a tenth of your spices—mint, dill and cummin. But you have neglected the more important matters of the law—justice, mercy and faithfulness. You should have practiced the latter, without neglecting the former" (Matt. 23:23). In this passage, Jesus reiterated several important principles of giving, and particularly the giving of the tithe, that are still applicable. (1) Giving includes the offering of a proportionate tithe, "You give a tenth." (2) Giving is an act of reverence and obedience to God's will and God's Word, "You have neglected the more important matters of the law—justice, mercy and faithfulness." (3) Giving is a duty that should not be neglected, "You should have practiced the latter, without neglecting the former."

Jesus also taught that the giving of tithes and offerings should come from a heart that is wholly devoted to God. He warned about giving tithes as a *display* rather than as an act of *devotion:*

> Two men went up to the temple to pray, one a Pharisee and the other a tax collector. The Pharisee stood up and prayed about himself: "God, I thank you that I am not like other men—robbers, evildoers, adulterers—or even like this tax collector. I fast twice a week and give a tenth of all I get."
>
> But the tax collector stood at a distance. He would not even look up to heaven, but beat his breast and said, "God, have mercy on me, a sinner."
>
> I tell you that this man, rather than the other, went home justified before God. For everyone who exalts himself will be humbled, and he who humbles himself will be exalted (*Luke 18:10-14*).

Jesus didn't reprimand the Pharisee for obeying the law of the tithe. In fact, His very mention of proportionate giving is evidence of Jesus' approval. He reprimanded him for putting this token of obedience on a pedestal instead of putting it in the offering basket.

The apostles were tithers.

"Now about the collection for God's people: Do what I told the Galatian churches to do. On the first day of every week, each one of you should set aside a sum of money in keeping with his income, saving it up, so that when I come no collections will have to be made. Then, when I arrive, I will give letters of introduction to the men you approve and send them with your gift to Jerusalem" (1 Cor. 16:1-3).

In New Testament times, Christians no longer brought gifts to a temple, they brought them to the church. In two New Testament accounts, Christians gave beyond the 10 percent and gave all that they had (Acts 2:44; 4:34). Today, the church argues for less than 10 percent. But the Early Church did more!

>〰️<

"God demands our tithes and deserves our offerings."
—Stephen Olford

Tithing helps the church. The church is commissioned to go into all the world and preach the gospel. It's a "great commission" that demands great support. Money is needed to print gospel literature, purchase television and radio airtime, build buildings, pay workers, and carry out countless other expenses associated with ministry. A tithing church will be able not only to pay its bills but also to expand its outreach. Tithing makes good sense.

But God also gives a caution to those who reject His call for proportionate giving. "Will a man rob God?" (Mal. 3:8). The verb "rob" here literally means "to cover" and thus to defraud and steal. "Robbing God" means keeping back from God what rightfully belongs to Him. A wise leader will faithfully present this truth to the congregation as a scriptural caution of God's judgment.

Bill Hybels teaches in his publications that, first and foremost, people "need to be taught that the tithe belongs to the Lord."

Tithing as an Investment

Tithing is not only a command of God but also one of the *opportunities* He offers His children. Tithing is good business. When we tithe, we go into business with God. He becomes our partner. It isn't 50-50, or even 90-10, however. God owns everything, and we are allowed to give 10 percent back to Him. In return, God promises to pour out a blessing. The money we give to God is not lost. We will see it again. God will return our investment here on earth and later in heaven.

Joe Seaborn said in a recent sermon, "The biggest beneficiary of consistent, methodical giving is yourself, myself. We develop a sense of inner integrity which only we and God alone can know, and that is the deepest satisfaction of all. When the Bible says that God honors those who honor Him (John 5:41-44), it means in a very practical sense, that as you share with God from the means He has given you, you will have a deep, God-anointed sense in your soul that you have done something with 'eternal righteousness' stamped on the side."

Jesus said, "Store up for yourselves treasures in heaven, where moth and rust do not destroy, and where thieves do not break in and steal" (Matt. 6:20). Jesus promises us that wealth can be sent ahead and accumulated in heaven. No miraculous accumulation of material riches was in mind. Christians can use their money to accomplish spiritual good, and God then credits it to the believer's account. God cannot forget a Christian who invests money to support missionaries, build churches, broadcast the gospel, or provide services where the lost are saved. At the judgment seat of Christ, following the rapture of the saints, rewards will be issued to those who have served God and Christ out of hearts of love (1 Cor. 3:11-15; 2 Cor. 5:10).

Some may question the motive of tithing as an "investment." They may say it is lustful. But it must be remembered that money is neutral. There is nothing inherently evil about money itself, and yet there are many who misquote 1 Tim. 6:10, "For the love of money is a root of all kinds of evil." Money is not the evil. *The love of money* is the source of all kinds of evil. The lust of money is evil. God returns to those who give in faith, not to those who give selfishly.

Don Marquis is quoted as saying, "There is nothing so habit-forming as money."[5]

"The greatest addiction today is the habit of accumulating money. We forget why we want it, what it is for, and what we are sacrificing for it. We don't need to give away our money, or not earn it, but we do need to give away our love for it."[6]

Dr. Samuel Young, former general superintendent of the Church of the Nazarene, once said, "Man needs a total God to serve Him fully in this present world, and in turn, God demands a total man as a channel for redemption's power running into every area of human life."

Money is life. The dollars in our wallet or purse represent the time we invest at our place of employment. Our paycheck is an exchange for giving ourselves to our job. The money we get represents our life. Therefore, we give part of our life when we place our offering in the offering plate.

Charles Swindoll wrote, "We honor God by first giving to Him from our paycheck. In doing so, we acknowledge His ownership of everything before we enjoy any of it ourselves. Whatever your income, give a portion to the Lord first. He will be honored and glorified by your trust."[7]

The story is told of one pastor who decided to finance the church in a way other than by giving the first portion. Creatively, the pastor wrote the congregation, "As all of you know, the church owns some two and a half acres of land that is currently vacant and doesn't plan to use them. For this reason, the finance committee has a new idea for financing the program of the church. If worked properly, it could be the answer to all of our financial problems. We will begin by investing in a possum ranch. It is our desire to start rather small, with just 250,000 possums. Each possum averages about 12 young possums a year. The skins can be sold for about $.40 for the gray ones and up to $.90 for the silver ones. This would give us 3,000,000 possum skins per year to sell at an average price of around $.75 each, making our revenue $2,250,000 per year. Think of the jobs we could provide! This actually averages out to $7,500 a day, excluding Sundays and holidays."

The preacher continued, "A skilled possum skinner can skin about 150 possums per day at a wage of $50, so it would take 150 people to operate the ranch for a net profit of $2,500 a day, or $750,000 a year. "Now," he says, "the possums would be fed on rats exclusively. Rats multiply four times as fast as possums so we could start a rat farm next to our possum ranch. If we start with 250,000, we will have four rats per possum, per day, and the rats will be fed on the carcasses of the possums that we skin. This will give each rat a quarter of a possum."

"Now you can see by this," the pastor said, "the business is a clean operation, self-supporting and truly automatic throughout. The possum will eat the rats, the rats will eat the possum, and we'll get the skins. Eventually, it is our hope to cross the possum with snakes, so then they'll skin themselves twice a year. This," he continued, "will save the labor costs for skinning, as well as giving two skins for one possum. What do you think?"

He added, "The alternative to this is for each one of us to take very seriously our responsibility and opportunity to help support the church and the spreading of the gospel. This would also solve all the money problems, and we are confident this is a plan that will find much more favor in the eyes of the Almighty." And he's right. There is a better way!

Joseph Stowell said in *Leadership Journal,* "Teaching people to give to God is an important part of a minister's responsibilities. Strong ministries producing saved souls and meaningful corporate worship are two strong (silent) influences toward increased giving. But money sometimes must be preached about."[8]

You might be a preacher if . . .

You've ever wanted to try multilevel tithing.

Stan Toler and Mark Toler-Hollingsworth, *You Might Be a Preacher If . . .* , vol. 2 (Tulsa, Okla.: Albury Publishing, 1998). Illustration by Cory Edwards. Used by permission.

Tithing to the Local Church

Storehouse tithing is God's commonsense way of growth. Everyone gives to the church, God's institution on earth, and together, enough money is gathered to preach the gospel and to help fulfill Christ's commission. Where does the principle of storehouse tithing come from? Several important biblical concepts must be understood:

God's Meeting Place

Throughout the Old Testament, God had a *place* for, (1) celebrating the symbols of redemption—the sacrificial offerings; (2) a central assembly where God met with people; (3) a location where the tithes and offerings were received. This principle continues in the New Testament. The church is God's place for, (1) celebrating the symbols of redemption—baptism and the Lord's Supper; (2) the central place where Christians assemble ("church" means assembly); (3) the place where the people bring their tithes and offerings.

The first "centralized presence of God" on earth was in the Tabernacle constructed by Moses at Sinai (Exod. 40:34-38). There, centralization of worship became very important to the people of Israel. God didn't intend for the Israelites to be bogged down by the idolatrous influences of Canaan, so He gave instruction to tear down heathen places of worship.

In place of those heathen worship sites, God instructed His people to meet at a specific and centralized site. The three purposes cited above are clearly observed in this passage:

> You must not worship the LORD your God in their way. But you are to seek the place the LORD your God will choose from among all your tribes to put his Name there for his dwelling. To that place you must go; there bring your burnt offerings and sacrifices, your tithes and special gifts, what you have vowed to give and your freewill offerings, and the firstborn of your herds and flocks. There in the presence of the LORD your God, you and your families shall eat and shall rejoice in everything you have put your hand to, because the LORD your God has blessed you (*Deut. 12:4-7*).

In the Old Testament, the Israelites were required to pay their tithe at "God's place"—the Tabernacle, and later the Temple. The purpose of paying the tithe was fourfold: (1) to worship God, (2) to support the Levites—the priests, (3) to provide for the maintenance of God's house ("God's place"), and (4) to prosper individually (Deut. 12:22).

The Altar of God

God also instructed the Israelites to bring an offering to the "place" and put it on the *altar.*

> When you have entered the land the LORD your God is giving you as an inheritance and have taken possession of it and settled in it, take some of the firstfruits of all that you produce from the soil of the land the LORD your God is giving you and put them in a basket. Then go to the place the LORD your God will choose as a dwelling for his Name and say to the priest in office at the time, "I declare today to the LORD your God that I have come to the land the LORD swore to our forefathers to give us." The priest shall take the basket from your hands and set it down in front of the altar of the LORD your God (*Deut. 26:1-4*).

The ceremony of giving was a reminder of God's promise to give them a land of inheritance. He promised them a land where they would till the soil and feed their flocks. Moses instructed Israel to give their offering as a symbol of the promise, and as a reminder to always give God the firstfruits of their harvests.

The Israelites were to give their tithes to the Levites, and then the Levites were to take a tithe of these offerings and give it to the priests. It should be noted that giving the tithe to the Levites is similar to our giving of tithes in the church today. The offering is received in the local church, and a portion is given to the ministry (in church denominations, that includes the general, district, and local church ministry).

God's Designated Storehouse

Although the Mosaic Law remained in effect for 15 centuries, from the time of Moses to the time of Christ's death at Calvary, the Jews often ignored, defied, or buried it beneath traditions. When their spiritual life was low, their giving fell off, and when they were spiritually revived, their giving rose again.

God sent prophets, such as Malachi, to warn them about their backslidings and invite them to return to Him. With their return, God promised to meet them in reconciliation.

"Ever since the time of your forefathers you have turned away from my decrees and have not kept them. Return to me, and I will return to you," says the LORD Almighty.

"But you ask, 'How are we to return?'

"Will a man rob God? Yet you rob me.

"But you ask, 'How do we rob you?'

"In tithes and offerings. You are under a curse—the whole nation of you—because you are robbing me. Bring the whole tithe into the storehouse, that there may be food in my house. Test me in this," says the LORD Almighty, "and see if I will not throw open the floodgates of heaven and pour out so much blessing that you will not have room enough for it" (*Mal. 3:7-10*).

No matter how Israel tried to rationalize their behavior, those who failed to bring their tithes and offerings to the designated place at the designated time were guilty of disobedience to God. Those who did all that was expected of them could feel confident they had obeyed the Lord.

In summary:

1. God has a special place for His children to bring their tithes and offerings. In the wilderness, the Israelites brought them to the Tabernacle. In the land of Canaan, they brought them to Shiloh, or Jerusalem. There, the crops and the animals were converted into cash and used to contribute at God's place.

2. **Today, the designated place is the local church,** if we follow through on the pattern laid down for taking contributions to the Tabernacle or to the Temple.

3. **What was once a voluntary custom of contributing tithes and offerings to the Lord, became a requirement** under the Mosaic Law. Christians today give their tithes because they are under grace. The pattern of giving 10 percent, and more, was established in ancient times as a guideline and the pattern continues in the church.

4. **Throughout the history of God's dealing with His people, their willingness to make contributions to His work depended upon their relationship to Him.** If they walked in close fellowship with Him, they supported His work gladly. When they rebelled against Him, they withheld their tithes.

5. **God is not destitute if we fail to give money to Him, but we are spiritually impoverished if we have no desire to give to Him.** The local church cannot survive and prosper unless we support it as we should. And further, unless we support it as we should, local churches cannot be planted on home or foreign mission fields.

Overcoming Negative Giving Attitudes

One day a pastor was summoned to the house of a parishioner who was having financial difficulties. The pastor counseled him for a while and then stopped. "Let's have a word of prayer and while I pray, you make a commitment to give one-tenth of your income to the Lord." Considering his income, the man thought to himself, "That won't be difficult. That's only $400 a year—only $8 per week." They prayed, and the man promised to give back 10 percent to the Lord and to the Lord's work. Years passed and the man's income greatly increased—to over $100,000 a year.

He called for the pastor once again. "Pastor, I'd like to be released from that 10 percent I promised the Lord several years back. A tenth of my income is now over $10,000 a year, and I have some plans for spending that."

"That's no problem," the preacher replied. "Let's pray." As they bowed their heads, the pastor began to pray, "Lord, You know what a problem this increase has been to my brother here. I'm asking you to reduce his income, perhaps back to the original $4,000, so he'll be able to afford his tithe once again . . ."

"Hold it!" the parishioner shouted. "That's not quite what I had in mind!"

As you begin to cast a vision for giving, you will encounter what Zig Ziglar might call *"Stinkin' Stewardship Thinkin'."* There are several negative attitudes that will have to be overcome by some of your congregation.

1. **Some will say, "I'm in debt. I can't give."** Many people feel that they are so far in a financial hole, that they cannot give a tithe to God. Remember, it was a wrong attitude that got them into debt in the first place. Because they made bad decisions, they ended up in debt. What will get them out? A right attitude. They must be challenged to begin giving their tenth to God, and then properly manage the remaining 90 percent until they are out of debt.

2. **Some will say, "I'll give more when I get more."** They think that if God will bless them, they will give more. However, more money won't change anything. Only a change of attitude and a new approach to money will produce more money. Their wrong attitude will keep them from getting additional money. In fact, their wrong attitude will keep them from *getting* more money, just as it will keep them from *giving* additional money. They need an adjustment in their attitude, not an adjustment in their wages.

3. **Some will say, "I can't give. I'm in debt because of circumstances."** They'll blame someone or something else. It's the boss's fault. It's the inflation or the recession. It's the spouse's spending habit. The question should be asked, "Who is responsible for your indebtedness?" "Are you in debt because of the layoff, or was it because of that new boat?" Obviously, some circumstances bring financial burdens. In that case, the Bible teaches the church to give a cup of cold water in the name of Jesus. But some people create their own poverty. Their cash flow may be all right but their "outgo" may be centered on "stuff." Their poverty may be a poverty of the soul. They need to see what the Bible says about priorities.

4. **Some will say, "I won't give. I'm mad!"** They're bitter because of their financial bondage. Whether or not they blame somebody else, their bitterness has robbed them of what little joy they had, with what little money they had. James the apostle asked, "What causes fights and quarrels among you? Don't they come from your desires that battle within you? You want something but don't get it. You kill and covet, but you cannot have what you want. You quarrel and fight. You do not have, because you do not ask God" (James 4:1-2).

**"Catch me when the sermon's over,
and we'll see if I'm still in the mood."**

5. **Some will say, "I'm not giving. I'm giving up!"** Some people only see "the system" and express their "couldn't care less" attitude. They've been on too many job interviews. They've filled out too many job applications. They don't look within, they just look around. They're like the workers in Jesus' parable who just stood around complaining because no one hired them. They're among those who ask some of those E-mail questions like, "Why do they call it a TV set when you only get one?" or, "How did a fool and his money get together in the first place?" Life is a lump in the gravy of their heart.

Or, you may launch an inventive scheme to overcome giving obstacles, like the pastor who announced over the sound system, from behind the platform, "Blue minivan, license number XYZ100, you've left your lights on and you've fallen behind on your stewardship pledge year-to-date."

There are more practical steps for casting your vision for a giving church. Among the most important is an understanding of the donor's motivation. Understanding what motivates people to support a church is invaluable, not only in raising funds for ministry, but also in getting a handle on people's values and priorities.

Build Positive Relationships with Key Givers

Sensitivity to the givers in each local church is essential. Pastors must learn to build strong relationships with each faithful giver. There are at least five key issues to keep in mind when building relationships with local church givers.

1. **Always seek to involve them in the ministries of the local church.** People who serve as lay ministers, as volunteers assisting in the church's operations, as members of boards, committees, or other decision-making bodies, or through hands-on interaction in the church ministry, are most likely to have a donor relationship to the church. George Gallup has been quoted as saying, "The church must investigate why people give. Does the church offer compelling reasons for its members to give? Parishes and dioceses should remember that financial giving is closely tied to gifts of time. People need to be involved with and care about an institution if they are going to support it financially."

2. **Communicate financial information frequently.** Relationship-building communications are personalized and targeted to the interests of the donor. They consider letters, newsletters, bulletins, and other publications to be symbols of their acceptance.

3. **Happy givers influence others to give.** One of the secrets in building donor loyalty is to encourage those who are already loyal to the church to bond with others who are interested. When church attenders discover that friends or respected members are givers, there is the potential for developing a "dual-level commitment"—loyalty to the church and loyalty to friends within the church.

4. **Acknowledge gifts to the local church in a timely manner.** Just as Jesus healed people and they felt a bond to Him afterward, many people perceive they have a relationship with a church after the church has served their needs in a tangible way. For example, many souls have been won to Christ through a church that has reached out to them in love during a crisis time in their lives. A note, family dinner, food shower, love offering, and so forth, have been "cords" that have drawn many people into a relationship with the church.

5. **Inform givers concerning special needs and ideas for growth.** It's one of the dominant motivations for giving to a church.

A "hot button" cause or idea may be just the thing to encourage giving to the church.

Creating a Climate for Giving

Once we understand some of the donors' motivations for giving to the church, we must proceed to the stage of planning to involve them. What practical steps should the leader take to create an environment that will give parishioners an incentive to give? Here are some suggested steps:

1. Offer regular classes on money management to potential givers. Larry Burkett said, "A family that finds itself unable to make a commitment of a tenth of its resources to God should realistically examine its spending and living habits. Perhaps that will require a crucial examination of spiritual values as well. Usually, if more funds are needed for family conveniences, the average family somehow finds the means to buy what they want."[9]

Maybe the reason that most baby boomers do not give more money to the church is because they're not only the wealthiest generation in the history of our country but also the most indebted. And with that debt hanging over them, they need the church to help them achieve financial freedom. What do they need to learn?

▷ They need to learn how to buy only what they can afford.

▷ They need to learn how to keep from guaranteeing what they're not prepared to pay.

▷ They need to learn how to use their wealth in worship.

▷ They need to learn how to use their wealth for their families.

▷ They need to learn how to use their wealth for those in need.

Pastor John Towler addressed the issue of debt in a message to his congregation, "Debt is not just a personal problem, it's a national problem. The United States of America has gone from being the largest creditor in the world to the largest debtor in the world. As a nation, we run an annual deficit of $400 billion a year." Then he outlined some steps for financial freedom:

1. *Establish a written budget.*

2. *Prioritize debts.*

3. *Accumulate no new debts.*

4. *Learn to be content with what you have.*

5. *Don't give up!*

I once heard Paul Tanner, executive secretary of the Church of God Council, say, "Our sense of values has been struck a devastating blow. We pay athletes millions and maintain missionaries at a poverty level. We spend more for tobacco than for education; more for booze than for all religion at home and around the world. Our churches are about empty on prayer meeting night and our penitentiaries are running over. We may not reasonably expect a pagan world to understand real value. The world is, after all, committed to itself, is focused on the temporary, and is under-equipped to handle anything of real substance."

Sadly, the church has not developed an immunity to some of the world's ailments. Some of our parishioners are doing "revolving" time in "plastic prisons" because they've been exposed to the "buy now, pay later" extortionists. Someone said, "Only in America do banks leave both doors open and then chain the pens to the counter." Our value system is in need of some spiritual surgery. The church, as well as the world, needs to understand what is value and what is a vacuum.

"Stewardship is not humanity's way of raising money, but rather God's way of raising people into the likeness of His Son."
—Doug Carter

Waldo J. Werning said, "Man is such an earthbound creature, often depending more on human eyes than on spiritual sight, who like an earthworm or snail, crosses roads and sidewalks which are filled with danger, instead of staying in the safe areas."[10]

By getting people to a point where they achieve financial freedom and are delivered from financial bondage, you will develop more givers, because they will have more dollars with which to work.

Make sure your ministry is "user-friendly." In a market-mentality age, people need to know that your church is interested in meeting needs. For example, a helpful seminar on handling finances from a biblical perspective will certainly be helpful to people living in the "money crunch." Resources from such authors as Ron Blue or Larry Burkett could be shared in that seminar. You could also do a small-group series from books like *Family Budget Matters* or *Mastering Your Money*. You don't have to be an expert; the materials have already been written. By sharing practical tips for financial freedom, your congregation will be encouraged to move forward in stewardship training.

2. Establish a vital mission and compassion ministry to others. There are whole denominations that have been started out of one person's deep compassion and concern for a lost world. As the church's ministry of compassion grows, the church grows. Gary Morsch writes, "At the time of the Reformation . . . meeting the needs of people was still largely intact. John Calvin reflected the prevailing practice of the time by advocating that one-fourth of all church income go to the poor in the congregation and one-fourth to others in need outside the church. Fully one-half of the church's income was to go to those in financial need."[11]

Once people have caught your church's vision for mission and ministry, they will seek to share in the plan—and probably will want to experience ministry "hands-on."

It's much like the young man who received a brand-new driver's license. The family bravely decided to take a ride with the new driver.

Dad immediately opened the backseat door and got in—directly behind the new driver. The young man surmised, "Dad, I'll bet you're back there seeing what it's like to ride in the backseat, after all those years of sitting up here behind the wheel."

The dad replied, "Nope! I'm sitting back here 'cause I'm gonna kick the back of the seat as you drive—just like you've been doing to me all these years!"

Years of people's refusal to share in ministry can bear fruit in one visionary moment. They'll "shine" in that inspired moment when they get a chance to practice the principles that have been preached to them. Assuredly, while some people will respond to that vision, others will miss it altogether.

For example, one church wanted to do something creative with their talents and their gifts. Two of the trustees had gone on a trip to Honduras to prepare for a work team that would be coming later. The host took them to a place where a hurricane had destroyed a church and said, "If there's any way you could find it in your heart to help rebuild this church, it would be such a blessing."

The pastor who had accompanied the trustees asked what the

project would cost. The host responded with a figure of $5,000. The pastor's own church was in the middle of a building project and was trying to raise its own funds, and the campaign hadn't been very successful. But on a Sunday morning, he felt impressed of the Lord to raise the $5,000 for the rebuilding project in Honduras. With inner confidence, the pastor announced to the congregation what he felt God wanted him to do, "I feel like we ought to give $5,000 to build this church."

To his surprise, a lady in the back of the auditorium stood and said, "Pastor, this is not right. Here we are diligently trying to raise money for building our own building, and now you're trying to raise money for a church in Central America. I don't understand why you're doing this, and I just want you to know that I'm against it!"

To his further surprise, he heard himself respond, "The Spirit just told me you're out of order. The Spirit is saying to me this needs to happen, and so, despite what has just been said, I'm going to pass the plates. Ushers, please come."

The offering plates were passed, and the amount given was $5,223. The pastor was vindicated, but little did he realize that there was a man listening to the service by radio. He was an alcoholic who had never been to church, but he heard the pastor raising the money for the Honduras project on the church's radio broadcast and admired him for it. The next morning, he went to see his attorney and advised him that he wanted to leave his entire estate to the church.

Little did he know that two weeks later he would die in a tragic fire. And, little did the church know that it would be the recipient of an estate that totaled $156,000. All because a pastor and congregation were willing to look beyond themselves, much like the Macedonians in the New Testament account, and give out of their own poverty.

The Lord has a wonderful way of bringing it back.

That incident was the impetus for the church's building of a new 1,300-seat sanctuary that they now worship in—debt free.

3. Challenge Christians to give through a vision plan that will prove God with their giving. Vision is providing people with a compelling portrait of the future to which they may then devote themselves. It must be promoted consistently and passionately by the primary leaders of the church and should stand as the core perspective from which ministry decisions are made.

Vision is the element that gives people hope for the future—

even if present conditions aren't satisfying. To encourage people to give generously, church leaders must provide a detailed and realistic picture of the future.

Again, Joe Seaborn said in a recent message, "We are not giving to make a treasurer happy, or to relieve the stress of the pastor, or to silence our conscience, or to give a tip to God. We are giving because in the overall pattern of Christian living, this is how God maintains His kingdom on earth, and we want to be part of that plan. We simply must see our giving in that grand light. Unless we do, we will never consistently give, no matter how strong a 'law' it may have been in the home where we grew up."

Rick Warren, author of *The Purpose-Driven Church,* led his church from infancy to 12,000 in attendance in 15 years! How? He's a *visionary* leader. He said at a conference in Oklahoma City, "God gave me a vision to build a purpose-driven church."

Warren recently raised $23.5 million in one weekend for a building project. He told the *Los Angeles Times,* "We exceeded all the goals that we had in mind. I've always eschewed fund-raising gimmicks and consultants, but as I've gone through this campaign, the greatest legacy will be our spiritual growth." He continued, "Instead of using traditional fund-raising approaches—bake sales, garage sales, and all of that—we designed a campaign that would teach six character qualities." Here are the qualities: Faith, Hope, Love, Sacrifice, Commitment, and Generosity.

Those qualities are supremely important in casting a vision for a giving church. They are the characteristics that must be developed in the church's leaders. And that development will be advanced by giving them a vision plan they can connect to.

Many pastors struggle with the "vision" thing. But every pastor who is making a difference in his or her community has a sense of destiny that is driven by the leadership of the Holy Spirit.

Vision is the key to making an impact for God in an unholy world.

Perhaps these simple steps will assist you in your search for a vision from God:

▷ Spend time daily in prayer, asking God to give you a vision for your church or ministry.

▷ Study the needs of your surrounding community or the people God has called you to reach.

▷ Seek wise counsel from visionary leaders.

▷ Examine your resources.

▷ Accept what God reveals to you and share it with your followers.

Henrietta Mears once said, "There is no magic in small plans. When I consider my ministry, I think of the world. Anything less than that would not be worthy of Christ nor of His will for my life."

Perhaps you've heard the story about the church member who was considering a gift to his church of over $100,000. He asked the pastor, "If you had some unexpected financial resources available, what would you do with them?" The pastor thought for a moment and then answered that he would like to rewallpaper the ladies' rest room. The man gave him $500 for the project—and ended up giving $99,500 to another ministry that had a vision big enough to worthily put his gift to work for Kingdom purposes.

Steps to a Vision Plan

Pastor Terry Toler was conversing with a little girl in the auditorium before the Wednesday night service. He asked how old the little girl was. She straightened out her little fingers and held them before her face, "I'm four."

"Four!" the pastor replied. "Are you going to have a birthday soon?"

"Yep, and then I'll be five," she announced.

And then there was a long pause, accompanied by a serious look on the little girl's countenance. She said, "And when I'm five, I'll learn to share."

"And why is that?" the pastor responded.

"Well," she added, "ya' know, it takes a long time to learn to share."

And church leaders must also be reminded that it may take awhile for their people to learn how to share. There is no quick fix to any major problem that faces a local church—especially when it comes to reversing years of giving (or lack of giving) habits.

It only stands to reason that "vision plans" will take some *planning*.

Step one is the mission. Why should your congregation give? What kinds of motivation for giving can you provide them? What is the specific cause that is to be represented? How significant or compelling is that cause to potential donors? Those are important questions to be considered as your vision plan unfolds. Your vision plan will be presented to a people who won't be involved *accidentally*. They will be people who will be involved *on purpose!* It would be wise for you to carefully—and prayerfully—consider that purpose by writing it out and reviewing it with trusted advisers.

Step two is the ministry. What is the immediate need? When people think about the ministry needs of the church, what will most readily come to their minds? Are those "needs" considered to be urgent? Will their involvement facilitate important changes or will it merely contribute to an organizational survival mode? What difference will it make?

Step three is the direction. How will the vision plan be communicated to the church? What steps will be taken to present a clear and informative presentation of the vision? What will the plan say about the future? How will it build upon the success of the past? Is it a plan that all the people can relate to?

Step four is the impact. What will be the benefits for those who get involved?

A pastor in Indianapolis wrote about looking the community over for a *need*. In a nearby rundown park, they discovered their *purpose*. The sign in front of their church said "A Church That Cares." With 65 in attendance, no one from the immediate community was coming to the church.

They took on the park renovation project and made it their *vision plan*. With volunteer labor from the church, sacrificial giving, and a spirit of *compassion*, they made their community park a beautiful place for people to meet and children to play.

Following the park project, the pastor began to teach biblical stewardship principles and the church began to grow. The pastor said, "Our church continues to experience incredible attendance and financial growth. Only God could bring these results. He sends His resources through His people."

It's true. *Whenever there's a need, God has prearranged a supply for His people.*

The pastor added, "Giving to the building fund is consistent. Last Sunday we received our Faith Promises for missions, and the response was incredible!" Here is a pastor who communicated a vision to the congregation that started with a park renovation need.

A small church with a vision plan began to think stewardship principles, and it exploded!

Another pastor started employing stewardship principles and experienced a 10 percent increase per year. Most churches that are growing today have an average of 1 percent annual growth (in finances and attendance). This church grew by 10 percent, simply by developing committed stewards.

Communicating Vision

"Vision" is specific. "Mission" is general. Mission is like a picture frame. For instance, a church's mission might be to seek and to save the lost. It might also include leading Christian believers into a deeper walk with Christ and preparing young men and women for Christian service.

What is the vision? The vision is, in fact, getting *specific about the mission.* Vision is the picture in the "picture frame" of mission. It's the photo of where you are going. If you develop goals and strategies for getting there (and your goals will always shape your strategy and your plan), you'll have a greater chance of achieving your mission.

Educate the Membership

Educate your congregation about the various facets of your vision. Look at a vision for Faith Promise giving, as has been mentioned. Faith Promise giving is an *act of faith,* a promise of God to give us a specific amount for world evangelization—weekly, monthly, or annual giving. The New Testament church in Macedonia certainly had a vision for faith promise giving.

"They gave as much as they were able, and even beyond their ability. . . . And they did not as we expected, but they gave themselves first to the Lord and then to us in keeping with God's will" (2 Cor. 8:3, 5).

Jesus was aware that people often hoarded money for future calamities. So He sought to reassure them. "I tell you, do not worry about your life, what you will eat or drink; or about your body, what you will wear. Is not life more important than food, and the body more important than clothes? Look at the birds of the air; they do not sow or reap or store away in barns, and yet your heavenly Father feeds them. Are you not much more valuable than they?" (Matt. 6:25-26).

By faith, we place our tithe in the offering plate, because we know God will provide our future needs.

A Faith Promise commitment indicates many things. In essence, it says you believe:

▷ World evangelization is vital to the mission of the church.

▷ The gospel can change lives.

▷ Giving, although important, is secondary to faith and prayer.

▷ God will help you pay the amount committed.

To communicate a Faith Promise giving vision you might talk about how the dollars will be used in world evangelization. Who will be helped? How will they be helped?

People need to be educated about the wise use of the material resources God has given them. Charles Swindoll said at a Promise Keepers' event, "Want a picture of wealth without wisdom? How about the lottery winner who squanders all his winnings at the racetrack trying to win even more money. Wealth needs wisdom to guide it. Otherwise, money is just another tool for foolishness."

Motivate Through Stories of Lives Being Changed

You'll not only need to educate your congregation through teaching, worship, publications, and other ways but also need to motivate them to a "winning cause." Mission dollars are often the easiest to raise because the congregation knows that *people* are involved. The church leader must do a better job of communicating the whole scope of the church's ministry. Sam Williams wrote in *Net Results* magazine, "Commitment is the cumulative result of good information, intensified relationships and explorative experience. The mistake leaders make is to move too quickly for a commitment and to believe they have it when they have won a vote or approval of a new plan."[12]

The church's primary motivation is always the reaching of lost souls with the gospel of the Lord Jesus Christ. Herb Miller wrote, "Preach and teach that the congregation's primary stewardship is to give the life-changing gospel of Jesus Christ to people who have not yet received it . . . This focus produces several results, including, (a) satisfaction in following Jesus' Great Commission; (b) replacement of giving units that move away from the community each year; and (c) the possibility that operating budget income and missions giving can rise."

Confidently Ask Your People to Give a Generous Gift

Give your congregation an opportunity to respond. You may want to say, "I need you to get involved in the process of giving. Will you help me in the process?"

After several days on the job, a new pastor went to his congregation with a financial need. Several families who were loyal to the previous pastor had left the church. Their departure created not only a numerical vacuum but a financial vacuum as well.

The treasurer expressed concern to the pastor during a board meeting. The pastor decided he would share the need with the congregation that Sunday and give them an invitation to help meet the need. "We need $2,400 to meet our expenses this week. I'm asking you to prayerfully consider that need as you give this morning," the preacher said as he received the offering.

After the service, the special offering was counted. The total was $1,700. The pastor and board members decided they would make it a matter of prayer. The invitation had been given, and now they were believing the Lord to meet the need through His people.

A lady who had just started attending the church approached one of the board members at the place where they both worked.

"You know," she said, "I haven't paid my tithes for a long time. I want to help with that financial need pastor told us about last Sunday."

Her check was for $3,000! The pastor gave the invitation. God met the need.

Celebrate the Generosity of Your People

People need to know how much their faithfulness in giving is appreciated. One local church publishes a stewardship letter. In it, the leadership celebrates the giving of the people with a reminder, "God promises rich rewards for those who align their lives with His will. We want you to experience the deep satisfaction and the abundant blessings that are sure to follow whenever people surrender their hearts and follow where His Son leads in the Kingdom."

You may ask, "How do I share my vision?" Try some of these methods:

▷ Vision Sunday

▷ Missions Banquet

▷ Stewardship Month

▷ Stewardship education in Sunday School and small groups

▷ Special emphases in the church publications

Many believers who attend the services in your church have, at best, a muddled and rudimentary understanding of stewardship. Even if their lives depended on it, they couldn't accurately describe God's principles regarding their stewardship responsibilities.

In spite of this inability, those believers aren't bad people. The fact that they attend church, occasionally read the Bible, typically pray to God during the week, and believe that their faith is an important part of their lives, suggests that they have more than just a passing interest in knowing and serving God. They cannot *accidentally* become good stewards.

They must catch a vision—your vision. They must be taught how to use their time, talent, and treasure to fulfill Christ's commission to the church. As someone once said,

"You may be God's messenger to His people regarding His will for them in giving. What an exciting thought!"

3

DEVELOPING COMMITTED STEWARD LEADERS

It is required that those who have been given a trust must prove faithful (1 Cor. 4:2).

><>><><

"God has given us two hands—one to receive with and the other to give with. We are not cisterns made for hoarding; we are channels made for sharing."

—Billy Graham

Two MOTHERS WERE TALKING IN THE FOYER of the church. One of the mothers, looking a bit frazzled, began to unload on her friend, "I just can't get my kids to do anything around the house. I end up doing all the work myself—the cleaning, the dishes, the laundry, the yardwork. I'm exhausted!"

Her friend looked her in the eye and said, "Maybe you should just stop doing everything and see what happens."

The statistics on laypersons who are actively participating in the ministry of the church are alarmingly lopsided. In most congregations, 20 percent of the people are doing 80 percent of the work, while the other 80 percent are doing only 20 percent of the work.

That may be attributed to the fact, according to George Barna, that 80 percent of ministers in America today are talking about lay ministry but only 20 percent of them are actually providing their people with opportunities to get involved in ministry.

That's where the mother mentioned above had failed her children. Instead of assigning tasks to her children and then expecting them to follow through, she simply decided to do it all herself. We will become burned-out workaholics if we try to do everything that needs to be done all by ourselves; we will become effective leaders only if we delegate the work to those who surround us.

Laypersons should be inspired and empowered to fulfill their personal ministry in and through their local church, and in the world; it is the responsibility of the clergy to enable and equip them. Lay ministry is not merely another program—it is a mind-set. And it is a primary biblical principle. "We are therefore Christ's ambassadors, as though God were making his appeal through us. We implore you on Christ's behalf: Be reconciled to God" (2 Cor. 5:20).

In his letter to the Ephesians, Paul writes, "For we are God's workmanship, created in Christ Jesus to do good works, which God prepared in advance for us to do" (2:10). And in 1 Pet. 2:5, 9 we are told, "You also, like living stones, are being built into a spiritual house to be a holy priesthood, offering spiritual sacrifices acceptable to God through Jesus Christ . . . you are a chosen people, a royal priesthood, a holy nation, a people belonging to God, that you may declare the praises of him who called you out of darkness into his wonderful light."

All of these verses point to the importance of every believer having a ministry in the family of God.

"One of the significant roles of the pastor is equipping the laity for ministry. If a pastor is able to understand the congregation's spiritual gift mix, and allow them to do what they are most passionate about, one of the areas in which much time will be spent is in training people to do ministry in the Body of Christ. Workshops and seminars on teaching Sunday School, personal evangelism, writing, social services, and so on, are a must when lay equipping becomes a part of local church ministry."[1]

In a *Money Smart* quotation, we see the importance of educating and equipping laypersons in the stewardship of their time and talents, as well as their treasure, "The common measure for all of us is to achieve balance between using our possessions and being controlled by them. To do this, we must establish that we serve Christ first, and all other considerations are secondary." That principle of responsibility is made even clearer in another of Jesus' parables recorded in the New Testament.

A Parable for Leaders

On Tuesday of the Lord's last week on earth, He was teaching in the Temple, and the chief priest and the elders questioned His authority. "'By what authority are you doing these things?' they asked. 'And who gave you this authority?'" (Matt. 21:23).

It was customary for the Jewish leaders to question anyone's authority who came into their turf teaching and preaching.

Jesus didn't answer them directly, as they had hoped. He answered their question with another question, "John's baptism—where did it come from? Was it from heaven, or from men?" (v. 25). The Jews discussed it and decided that if they said the baptism came from God, Jesus would tell them they should have followed John. If they said it came from men, the people would turn against them, because John was considered to be a prophet from God.

Obviously Jesus had the Jewish leaders over a barrel. They didn't know what to say. "Neither will I tell you by what authority I am doing these things" (v. 27).

But Jesus didn't leave them frustrated. He gave them the parable of the two sons.

"There was a man who had two sons. He went to the first and said, 'Son, go and work today in the vineyard.' 'I will not,' he answered, but later he changed his mind and went. Then the father went to the other son and said the same thing. He answered, 'I will, sir,' but he did not go. Which of the two did what his father wanted?" "The first," they answered. Jesus said to them, "I tell you the truth, the tax collectors and the prostitutes are entering the kingdom of God ahead of you. For John came to you to show you the way of righteousness, and you did not believe him, but the tax collectors and the prostitutes did. And even after you saw this, you did not repent and believe him" *(vv. 28-32)*.

Equal Opportunity, Equal Responsibility

The parable speaks of stewardship—the stewardship of human responsibility, managing resources of time, talent, and treasures for the glory of God. Notice that both sons had equal opportunity and responsibility.

1. Both sons had the same relationship to the father. Jesus doesn't indicate that either son was the firstborn, just the first that the father approached with the responsibility. In the same sense, every believer has a responsibility to his Heavenly Father for stewardship. The Father comes to all of us, and we are all expected to obey.

Some might think that the younger believer can be disobedient, while the more mature believer must be instant in obedience. Because both are children of the Heavenly Father, both are expected to obey His command.

As a leader, your spiritual gifts may give you more usability, meaning one person may have 1 talent, while another person has 10 talents. Then, the persons with the most talents are accountable for more results, because they have more gifts. But every "son" is accountable for obedience, because God is the owner of all things.

2. Both sons had the same opportunity of inheritance. The father went to both sons and asked them to work on the farm. By increasing the father's assets, that would make the estate of both sons larger. So, each son had a stake in the work he was asked to do. Each would receive more, because they had the same inheritance opportunity. In the same manner, we serve our Heavenly Father because we are His children. John wrote, "To those who believed in his name, he gave the right to become children of God" (John 1:12).

Because you are God's child, you have access to the inheritance from Him. In that sense, you ought to work as diligently as you can to serve the Father in your leadership capacity.

3. Both sons had access to the same resources. They were not hired hands. Both sons had equal access to the tools on the farm. Because they were the sons of the farmer, they could have gone to the toolhouse and gotten anything they needed to get the job done. Good tools make your work easier and help you produce more.

Also, both sons had access to the family table. They were not hired hands who sat on the back porch to eat lunch. They sat at the same table with their father, enjoying the same food as their father.

And both sons had access to the father, for information and solution to their problems. Because the father is the owner of all things, he made the farm prosper. The sons are in a "growth mode." Since they don't know as much as the father, they can go and ask their questions and get solutions.

In equal manner, every Christian leader can "ask" because Jesus has promised, "The Father will give you whatever you ask in my name" (John 15:16).

4. Both sons had the same command. The father said to the first, "Son, go and work today in the vineyard." It was a direct and straightforward command. The second son received the same command.

Likewise, the children of the Father, and leaders in particular, have the same obligation of stewardship. We are all told to be holy in character (1 Pet. 1:17) and diligent in our work (Col. 3:23). In this sense, the Father has given every believer the same command, no matter how many talents they have.

5. Both sons had the same time frame. *Work today.* One son wasn't given the easy task of working in the morning, while another was asked to work in the heat of the midday. One son wasn't asked to work in the spring planting, while the other was to work in the harvest of the fall. They were both given the same time frame. They were both told to go to work immediately!

God has given every leader the responsibility of stewardship. Leaders are to manage what they have *today.* The Christian life is not "Spring Training," where the games don't count. What you manage today is being evaluated by the Father. God does not give you a mulligan shot as the beginning golfer might take. Every shot counts, and God expects all of us to obey Him—*today!*

Two Sons, Two Different Responses

Notice the response of the two sons, especially as it relates to stewardship. Their response is divided into two halves. The first half has to do with acknowledgment, and the second half has to do with actions. When God gives directions, He expects a twofold response. First, we are to acknowledge that He owns the farm, that He can give us directions and expect certain standards. When we make Jesus Christ the Lord of our life (Rom. 10:9-10), we acknowledge His *control* over our lives.

The second response is action. When the Father gives a command, He expects certain actions. The farmer expected the sons to use their abilities in the vineyard. The Heavenly Father expects His children to be workers. The song says, "In the harvest field now ripened, there's a work for all to do."

The first son responded with a "No!" We don't know why. Perhaps he felt inadequate for the work. Perhaps he felt the work was too demeaning. Perhaps he was lazy. Whatever the case, the first son didn't acknowledge his father's rightful ownership, directions, or inheritance. The Bible says, "Later he changed his mind and went." The first son repented, moving from a "no" to a "yes" as an act of the will. There are some modern stewards who have said no to God in their giving and in their service who need to repent and surrender to God's ownership.

The second son said, "Yes, Sir!" but didn't carry out the command. Jesus said, "Many will say to me on that day, 'Lord, Lord, did we not prophesy in your name' . . . Then I will tell them plainly, 'I never knew you'" (Matt. 7:22-23). Acknowledging without acting on His commands is rebellion.

God is calling leaders to do more than acknowledge Him. He is calling them to action—to be stewards of *His relationship, His inheritance, His resources, and His time frame.*

In *The Christian's Guide to Worry-Free Money Management,* authors Daniel D. Busby, Kent E. Barber, and Robert L. Temple illustrate the principle very well with a story about John Dewey.

"It is said that the philosopher John Dewey heard a commotion from the upstairs of his house and ran up the stairway to discover that the bathtub had overflowed. There his son stood, bewildered, as Dewey began to ponder how the overflow had ever happened.

"'Dad,' he said, 'This is not the time to philosophize. It's time to mop!'"[2]

> ## "A great leader takes people where they don't really want to go, but ought to be."
>
> —Rosalyn Carter

Three Types of Leaders

There are three types of leaders. **First, there is the servant leader.** The servant leader says, "I won't have any head tables." "I'll go last in line." "I will be a servant." The servant leader is more comfortable with a towel than a trophy.

The servant leader is sensitive to the hurts of others. Like the Good Samaritan, a servant leader stops to bind the wounds. No cost is too great for the healing of a fellow traveler.

The servant leader is sensitive to the feelings of others. If making waves would cause someone to shipwreck, the servant leader would rather not launch the boat. Feelings take precedence over the facts. Souls are worth more than statistics.

The servant leader is sensitive to the restoration of others. He or she frequently becomes burdened over divisions. The servant leader will bridge chasms of confusion with a word or action that will attempt to heal the disturbance. The servant leader prefers crow sandwiches to chicken dumplings, if it means peace at the table.

There's a story of a man who dreamed he died and stood in line at the Pearly Gates—beside his best friend. Suddenly, St. Peter appeared and announced, "I'm sorry. There's only room for one more." "I'll have to give you a test," he said, as he looked at the two applicants. "Which one of you is more humble?"

They both failed for various reasons.

The servant leader wouldn't fail. He or she has a heart for God and a mind like Christ, who said to His disciples, "If anyone wants to be first, he must be the very last, and the servant of all" (Mark 9:35).

The second is the shepherd leader. Most pastors and key laypersons adopt this model. They spend most of their time caring for others. H. B. London, at a recent Focus on the Family seminar for pastors, said, "Eighty percent of pastors are chronically fatigued because they spend all their time caring for others." Most lay leaders fall into this category and are fatigued because they're doing everything for the congregation.

A shepherd leader would, more than likely, post a sign-up sheet on the bulletin board for volunteers to clean the church, and then put his or her name at the top—or in any subsequent vacant space. The servant leader would polish every pew, scrape every snowflake, light every light, park every pickup, peel every potato, flip every flapjack, and commit to every committee, if it meant the spiritual welfare of another. Often their busyness is a prelude to burnout.

Dads and moms can be effective shepherd leaders. They often encourage their children to sign up for science projects and then work side-by-side with them to make sure the projects are completed. When their "little darlings" get too tired, they tuck them into bed with a lullaby, and stay up past the test pattern on the TV to get the project in on time. Little Johnny or Susie may get a good night's sleep and an A on his or her report card but will fail to learn a very important life lesson on the stewardship of time.

No matter the return, and no matter the personal consequence, the shepherd leader will seek the welfare of others. The job description of the shepherd leader is found in Christ's own words, "The Son of Man did not come to be served, but to serve, and to give his life as a ransom for many" (Matt. 20:28).

The Winning Combination

Perhaps the best model of leadership is found in the combination of the "servant leader" and the "shepherd leader," resulting in the third type of leader—the "steward leader." The steward leader becomes *a spiritual coach for the congregation.* In the field of athletics, the coach's great delight is to train an athlete to accomplish his or her "personal best." To do that, a coach must use a balance of education and encouragement, correction and praise, expectation and understanding, humility and courage. The steward leader learns how to model the very best of those qualities because they are best seen in *the* coach—Coach Jesus.

In athletics, the coach must be willing to be all things to the player—father, mother, sibling, or friend—to encourage a winning spirit and cultivate the best performance. A coach knows the needs of the players. For example, a coach knows when a player needs a word of correction, not for the sake of correction itself but for the welfare and discipline of the athlete. A coach also knows when a word of acceptance and affection is due for those who feel rejected or who have suffered a loss. The wisdom writer points to the greatest Friend, "There is a friend who sticks closer than a brother" (Prov. 18:24). Jesus described that friendship, "Greater love has no one than this, that he lay down his life for his friends. You are my friends if you do what I command. I no longer call you servants, because a servant does not know his master's business. Instead, I have called you friends, for everything that I learned from my Father I have made known to you" (John 15:13-15).

The steward leader seeks to emulate those qualities of friendship—love, loyalty, kind correction, and sacrifice—for the encouragement of others.

Another characteristic of coaching is respect. Great coaches don't command the respect of their players, they earn it. One of the greatest football coaches of all times was the late Vince Lombardi. It is said that he was such a friend to his players, and so revered by his players, that they would do anything possible to accomplish his objectives. One lineman said of Lombardi, "If he said 'Sit down!' I wouldn't even look for a chair!" Steward leaders earn the respect of those they lead. They understand how to bring out the best in others, not by coercion or manipulation, but by administration and instruction.

A coach also knows that the way to develop a winning team is not to be on the field for every play. Some teams do have "player coaches," but even the player coach knows when to sit on the sidelines and let the team members learn for themselves. The steward leader knows when to be a player and when to sit on the sidelines. The role of the coach is primarily that of an educator-encourager— knowing that a "Good job!" is sometimes more valuable to a player than good pay. This leader understands what it is to be a "manager of managers." Steward leaders are "steward managers." Their job is to get God's best resources out of God's people.

The armed forces have a category of duty known as "active reserve." Active reservists are people trained and ready for combat, but they are doing something else while waiting for the call. Some of them were *once* on the front lines. Some have been sidelined for various reasons. Others are well-trained but don't have enough experience. The steward leader is one who calls the "active reserves" of the church into full-blown, active duty.

The steward leader has a Spirit-filled heart and a Christ-filled agenda. Like the Sunday School scholar, the steward leader can sing "Jesus and others and you, / what a wonderful way to spell **JOY**." The steward leader is humbled by the spiritual growth and the active Christian service of those under his or her care.

"Leadership is both something you are and something you do."
—Fred Smith

Levels of Responsibility

Two levels of responsibility are critical to the steward leader:

Level one is leadership in the mission of the church. The steward leader is responsible to see that the message and the purpose of the church are carried out—and they know it well enough to effectively communicate it to others. That purpose may be spelled out in a formal "statement of purpose" or it may be assumed by the character of ministry emphases of the individual church.

The architecture of a building often reflects its mission and program. A more stately building, for example, suggests a more formal mission for that organization. Using the building analogy, some congregations naturally fall into architectural/mission categories.

Some are *lighthouses*. Their primary function/mission is to send out a beacon of salvation to their community by aggressive evangelism programs. They emphasize the training of laypersons to lead people to Christ through learned gospel presentations. They conduct regular community outreach campaigns, and they would be the first to sign up for a community-wide crusade by an itinerant evangelist.

Hospital churches are known to have a heart for the hurting. Their mission is to care for the walking wounded of the world, and it is evident in all of their programming. You will probably find a counseling ministry—with a paid counseling staff in some cases—in a *hospital* church. They are known in the community as a place where people can come to find solace for their sorrow.

Schoolhouse churches are characterized by their teaching emphasis. Their people carry notebooks along with their Bibles. Their bulletin is a virtual catalog of classes, class times, and class locations. *Schoolhouse* churches emphasize Bible memorization and reward the "memorizers" accordingly. The Sunday morning message may sound more like a classroom lecture than an evangelistic sermon in the *schoolhouse* church.

Concert hall churches emphasize performances. Their ministry focuses on polished presentations of the claims of Christ in music and dramas, as well as in dynamic preaching. They are known in the community as the church where the concert and recording artists make their scheduled stops. Their services are enhanced by the best in lighting, sound, and staging. Christmas and Easter programs in *concert hall* churches draw thousands, and many of their meeting times are spent in rehearsal for the next performance.

Retreat center churches emphasize prayer. The very architecture of their building lends itself to quiet solitude and reflection. And their ministry focuses on prayer—particularly intercessory prayer. Their bulletin boards are filled with pictures of missionary families. Their doors are usually open for personal prayer times, and they will dot their altars with 3" x 5" cards and prayer request containers. They host the community "concert of prayer." They identify with Jesus' words, "My house will be called a house of prayer for all nations" (Mark 11:17).

Then, there are some churches that may fit all the categories, in one way or another—they have a holistic approach to ministry. Their mission is so varied that it incorporates the best—and sometimes the worst—of all church ministry emphases. The steward-leader understands the particular mission of his or her church with all of its unique characteristics, and seeks to cast a vision for its spiritual, numerical, and financial growth.

"Vision" is discussed in the book *The People Principle: Transforming Laypersons into Leaders:*

> The primary enemy to church growth is clinging to tradition. This occurs when church leaders start living in the past rather than looking to the future. Lyle Schaller recently said, "Every day, seven churches in America close their doors and die." The only way to reverse this problem is to return to the vision for your church. When questions erupt—return to the vision. When doubts arise—return to the vision. When leaders stand opposite of one another—return to the vision. When attendance declines —return to the vision.

> Not long ago, comedian George Burns died at age 100. For years he had said, "I can't die—I'm booked until I'm 100!" But, with no more bookings, George Burns died. When churches run out of purpose, they die![3]

Level two is the stewardship of the gifts of God's people. It is the steward leader's responsibility to see that the gifts of fellow believers are used to their best advantage. The steward leader understands that everyone is a steward of a God-given ability that needs to be discovered, nurtured, and activated for the edifying of the Body of Christ.

That stewardship includes all areas of life, not just money. The church depends on steward leaders not only to use their dollars wisely but also to be available to help—using their own unique personalities and abilities. The steward leader also seeks to get others involved in ministry, in the very same way.

The result is capturing the congregation's imagination, and subsequently their responding with gifts of support for the local church.

"To grasp and hold a vision—that is the essence of successful leadership."
—Ronald Reagan

Qualities of Steward Leaders

1. **Steward leaders acknowledge the Lordship of Christ.** Committed steward leaders acknowledge the Lordship of Jesus Christ in all areas of their lives. As Dr. Roy S. Nicholson once said, "If He is not Lord of all, He will not be Lord at all." Steward leaders know that they are created in the image of God and that God is their source for everything. Steward leaders have resigned as "general manager of the universe" and have given God total control of their lives and their ministries.

2. **Steward leaders build winning relationships.** Just as successful coaches have an ability to relate to players, steward leaders concentrate on building winning relationships with people. They understand teamwork. They know that the Body of Christ is made up of unique and individual parts that work in cooperation with the Head, Jesus Christ. They know that relationships must be nurtured. And they possess **biblical character traits,** such as those recommended to the Christians in Rome by the apostle Paul:

> Love must be sincere. Hate what is evil; cling to what is good. Be devoted to one another in brotherly love. Honor one another above yourselves. Never be lacking in zeal, but keep your spiritual fervor, serving the Lord. Be joyful in hope, patient in affliction, faithful in prayer. Share with God's people who are in need. Practice hospitality.
>
> Bless those who persecute you; bless and do not curse. Rejoice with those who rejoice; mourn with those who mourn. Live in harmony with one another. Do not be proud, but be willing to associate with people of low position. Do not be conceited (*Rom. 12:9-16*).

Notice these biblical character traits in the scripture passage:

▷ **Sincerity.** "Love must be sincere." The steward leader will avoid manipulation of any kind. Management by coercion has no place in biblical leadership. The disciples didn't follow Jesus because they were forced to. They followed Him because of His sincere love for them and because of the sincerity of His mission.

▷ **Spirituality**. "Hate what is evil; cling to what is good." "The church is in need of more models than critics," someone once said. Those who would seek to lead others would be well-served to keep the principles outlined in a familiar Sunday School chorus, "Be like Jesus, this my song, / in the home and in the throng; / be like Jesus all day long, / I would be like Jesus." Team members who know their leader is wholly devoted to Christ are more willing to make greater efforts. And steward leaders who take their strength from a daily reading of God's Word and from daily prayer are those who find greater strength for the task.

▷ **Loyalty**. "Be devoted to one another in brotherly love." The late country singer Tammy Wynette gave the world a lesson in song that has been subject to much discussion, "Stand by your man." Steward leaders should be devoted to their team. Others may criticize them, but their leader won't. They will find positive characteristics in them and build a Christ-inspired loyalty around those characteristics. One of the greatest loyalty lessons in Scripture is given in the account of Jesus' meeting with the apostle Peter after the Resurrection. Jesus overcame the negative actions and reactions of the apostle with an appearance to him and an encouragement to forget the past and to "get back to work" ("feed my sheep").

▷ **Empathy**. "Honor one another above yourselves." Steward leaders have learned to "walk a mile in someone else's moccasins." They seek to understand the motives behind the actions of their team members. They look behind the Sunday morning "masks" and see the tears, as well as the triumphs of their workers.

▷ **Fervency**. "Never be lacking in zeal, but keep your spiritual fervor, serving the Lord." Steward leaders know that enthusiasm is more caught than taught. A leader who possesses some excitement about his or her task is a leader who will soon lead some excited followers. Enthusiasm is contagious.

▷ **Flexibility**. "Be joyful in hope, patient in affliction, faithful in prayer." Steward leaders understand that "one-size-fits-all" doesn't work in church ministries that are made up of so many different personalities. They also understand that their team members come from various environments and home backgrounds that have greatly affected them. Steward leaders learn to build personal ministries around the unique personalities of their team and avoid squeezing them into a programmed mold.

▷ **Generosity**. "Share with God's people who are in need." A steward leader who will go the extra mile is one who models the greatest leader—Jesus Christ. John 3:16 is still the greatest example of a loving and giving heart the world will ever see. Steward leaders who will be like Christ will be people of a generous spirit. That generosity will be seen not only in their giving but also in their leading.

▷ **Proximity**. "Practice hospitality." Steward leaders understand that one of the keys to building relationships with people is to spend time with them. They use meeting and planning times as building times. They also arrange for informal and relaxing times. Their friendliness, personal concern, and encouragement are characteristics that win people to them.

▷ **Stability**. "Bless those who persecute you; bless and do not curse." Steward leaders who learn to keep their cool in a calamity are leaders who will greatly influence their team members to personal excellence. Often, the team simply reflects the strengths or weaknesses of the coach. Hall of Fame basketball player and NBA coach Larry Bird exemplified stability in his rookie coaching assignment. Bird said he was determined to not be a coach who would rant and rave from the sidelines over the actions of players or refs, but rather he would be a coach who showed leadership in his restraint. That strength—stability—was seen in the coach's reactions when his team went to the NBA finals in his first year. His stoicism was the subject of more than one sports column and the subject of more than one photograph. He showed stability by not overreacting in a moment of crisis.

▷ **Humility**. "Do not be proud, but be willing to associate with people of low position. Do not be conceited." An elementary school girl came home from an all-school track meet and reported to her mother that she had won first place in the 100-yard dash.

"Where's your ribbon," her mother asked?

"I gave it away," the girl replied.

"You gave it away?" the surprised mom responded. "I thought you would have liked to hang that ribbon in your room, along with some of your other trophies."

"Well, Mom," the girl replied, "it's like this. There was a little girl in that race who ran the best she could but she didn't win a ribbon. She felt bad, so I gave her mine.

"And besides that," the little girl added, "I don't need a ribbon. I know I won!"

Steward leaders don't need ribbons to know they are winners. Their humble and generous spirit not only characterizes them as winners but reaches out to others and makes winners out of them as well!

3. Steward leaders are forward-thinking. Two golfers were discussing their scores after a round of golf. One of the golfers commented, "I have been playing golf for 20 years, and I get worse every year. Believe it or not, last year I played worse than the year before. And the year before, I was worse than the last year."

The other golfer responded, "That's too bad! How are you doing now?"

His friend answered unhappily, "I am already playing next year's game!"

Steward leaders are always "pressing toward the mark." For example, steward leaders may set a goal to grow in the service of giving. They know that it will be a process and that it will be hard work! As another example, steward leaders may determine to develop an attitude of spiritual gratitude. They determine that every time God blesses them, they will look for a way to bless someone else. Steward leaders are always seeking to reach their highest potential.

"While I believe in the 'God of the harvest,' I must first believe in the 'God of the seedtime.' The seedtime of God is sure. He always places a significant potential within us."

—Millard Reed

4. Steward leaders worship through giving. One pastor asks his leaders to put something into the offering plate every Sunday—even if they pay their tithes in one lump sum, one check during the month. He wants them all to bring their envelopes and get their family members, as much as they can, to participate. So whenever an offering plate is passed, the leaders participate. They are serving as role models for the entire congregation. Giving to God reminds the steward leader of who He is, who they are, and what their relationship should be to the things He has allowed them to manage in His name. Giving is done in love with a thankful and willing heart, all the time recognizing God as the owner of everything.

5. Steward leaders are mission-minded. Steward leaders say with John Wesley, "The world is my parish." They understand that Christ's commission includes not only their city, state, and region but also their world. Steward leaders are mission-minded. They take a proactive role in reaching the unreached with the gospel. They set an example with their faith promise giving. But they also know that the mission field is just as much across the street as it is across the sea. A quote from *Global Digest* in a local church's missions publication is great incentive to the steward leader's global vision, "We are so easily overawed by the scope of the Great Commission that our resolve weakens and our courage fails. But God is greater than His commission, greater than His earth, greater than any obstacles we will face. And though His *power* regards the nations as 'worthless and less than nothing,' His *love* regards them as infinitely precious and worthy of the death of His Son."

Leaders model excellence and quality.

A leader:

Maintains the mission

Oversees the plan

Develops more leaders

Encourages the heart

Loves to celebrate[4]

It's my latest invention! This offering plate will ring a little bell if you put in $20 . . . if you don't put in anything, it takes your picture.

© Mary Chambers. Used by permission.

6. Steward leaders model giving. Dr. Melvin Maxwell once said, "Whenever you ask for a dollar, give a dollar." It's a powerful principle. Steward leaders invite others to join them in a cause. Their gift makes a difference in the lives of others who see their participation, and they model their giving. An Oklahoma City attorney and newspaper columnist, Jim Priest, told of the dilemma that one well-known politician faced when it was discovered that he only gave $300 to charitable organizations in one year. Priest said, "In an era where 'looking out for No. 1' is a popular sentiment, it is absolutely imperative for our leaders—and our families—to display a giving spirit."

"A visionary leader commits to the vision."
—Jerry Falwell

The Steward Leader Parable

Jesus taught about the steward leader's responsibilities in a parable given in the Temple during the week of His crucifixion.

"Listen to another parable: There was a landowner who planted a vineyard. He put a wall around it, dug a winepress in it and built a watchtower. Then he rented the vineyard to some farmers and went away on a journey. When the harvest time approached, he sent his servants to the tenants to collect his fruit.

"The tenants seized his servants; they beat one, killed another, and stoned a third. Then he sent other servants to them, more than the first time, and the tenants treated them the same way. Last of all, he sent his son to them. 'They will respect my son,' he said.

"But when the tenants saw the son, they said to each other, 'This is the heir. Come, let's kill him and take his inheritance.' So they took him and threw him out of the vineyard and killed him.

"Therefore, when the owner of the vineyard comes, what will he do to those tenants?"

"He will bring those wretches to a wretched end," they replied, "and he will rent the vineyard to other tenants, who will give him his share of the crop at harvest time" (*Matt. 21:33-41*).

In this parable, Jesus makes three statements that apply to the steward leader.

First, God is the owner of all things, and His followers are stewards who are given the responsibility to manage His resources.

Second, the steward has the freedom to use his talents, resources, and circumstances to get the best results for the owner.

Third, the owner ultimately returns and asks to examine and reward the management of his stewards.

><><

"Leadership is the ability to organize the spiritual gifts and limitations of others."

—J. Osward Chambers

The Owner's Assignment

In Jesus' parable, the owner had a vineyard and he did many things to get his vineyard ready for harvest. **First**, he planted vines. **Second**, he put a wall around the vineyard to keep out animals, strangers, and any other threat to the vines. **Third**, he dug a winepress where the grapes could be squeezed and prepared. **Fourth**, he built a tower that provided water, via irrigation, to the vineyard. As far as the owner was concerned, he had done everything possible to guarantee a harvest of grapes.

The steward leader must first understand that God works in the hearts of individuals to bring them to salvation and then to Christian growth. The planting of the vine is like the sowing of the seed of the Word of God (Mark 4:14). Since the Word of God convicts us, the hard heart is broken by the Word of God. The first thing God does is to bring the Word of God to our hearts. That Word is an instrument of regeneration (i.e., we are born again by the Word of God) (1 Pet. 1:23).

The next thing the owner did for his vineyard was to prepare a wall to keep out varmints, those who would trample the seed, or any other problem that would keep the vine from growing. God brings circumstances in our hearts to bring us to salvation. "God's kindness leads you toward repentance" (Rom. 2:4). God is good to us. The sun shines on the just and the unjust to show His loving-kindness. He puts a wall about us to keep us from all types of danger. Why? Because of His mercy, He wants to give us an opportunity to say yes to Him.

The third thing the owner did was to dig a winepress, a place where the grapes are squeezed into wine. In this situation, God brings us to the place of conversion. We are presented with the gospel, either by natural revelation (Ps. 19:1) or by a presentation of God's special revelation (i.e., His Son who came to save us as seen in the Word of God).

The fourth thing the owner did was to build a tower, to provide irrigation and water for the continued growth of His vines. God has provided the ministry of the Holy Spirit to give us direction, fill us with power, and give us wisdom in the circumstances of life.

The owner does all of this in order that he might have fruit.

The Stewardship of the Vineyard

The Bible says the owner "rented" the vineyard to someone who wanted to till the ground and operate the vineyard for him. The owner did not do it himself but gave the stewardship of the vineyard to another.

In the same sense, **the steward leader must understand that God does not force His great purpose on the world. He does His work through people**—He gives them stewardship over His great purpose. Steward leaders carry out His work in the world. He has planned that His *work* would be done through His *workers*. The apostle Paul said, "We are God's fellow workers" (1 Cor. 3:9).

The Care of the Vineyard

The owner gave specific instruction for the care of the vineyard and for the harvest. God is in the world today, but many people do not see Him. Some try to put Him on the spot, "If I could see a miracle happen before my very eyes, I would believe." But God does not do "sign miracles" so that we may see the sign to believe. God has given us His Word, the Bible, and we are to believe through His Word. "Faith comes from hearing the message, and the message is heard through the word of Christ" (Rom. 10:17). God has determined that there are certain means by which people will come to salvation. He does not whisper audibly into ears, He does not show His face on a dark night, nor does He do other outward phenomena to draw people to himself.

The steward leader must be a student and a teacher of God's Word. God has revealed His will for individual lives, and His will for the corporate Body of Christ, the Church, through the Scriptures.

The Owner's Departure

Just as in the story, the owner departed, so Jesus Christ went back to heaven at the Ascension and is at the right hand of God the Father in glory. At times, His departure might seem to be a time of silence. But even when God seems to be silent, He speaks to us: through nature, through His Word, and through the evidence of the Holy Spirit. God is never far away in His *presence* or in His *promises*. The apostle gives us a glimpse,

> Paul, a servant of Christ Jesus, called to be an apostle and set apart for the gospel of God—the gospel he promised beforehand through his prophets in the Holy Scriptures regarding his Son, who as to his human nature was a descendant of David, and who through the Spirit of holiness was declared with power to be the Son of God by his resurrection from the dead: Jesus Christ our Lord. Through him and for his name's sake, we received grace and apostleship to call people from among all the Gentiles to the obedience that comes from faith. And you also are among those who are called to belong to Jesus Christ (*Rom. 1:1-6*).

The owner (Christ) will come back to settle things that now look unsettled. Those "who are called to belong" will one day be "called away" in the twinkling of an eye. On that day, every earthly account will be settled. One great gospel preacher used to proclaim, "Payday Someday!" **The steward leader must understand that God sees his or her work and will reward it accordingly.** The writer to the Hebrews made a spectacular promise to weary Christians burdened down by their times, their labor, and their search for spiritual meaning in the spiritual ceremonies of their day, "God is not unjust; he will not forget your work and the love you have shown him as you have helped his people and continue to help them" (6:10).

"The harvest time approached" (Matt. 21:34). The owner knew when it was time to harvest the vineyard. In the same way, God knows when the final harvest, the second coming of Jesus Christ, will be fulfilled. For the workers, the time of harvest meant **(1) a time of compensation.** Their every effort would receive a full recompense of reward. The steward leader must keep the hope of Christ's coming alive in his or her heart. For the worker, the time of harvest also meant (2) **a time of completion.** As in every job there is a payday, so for every task there is a completion. Jesus had a sense of urgency in His ministry on earth (John 9:4-5). Likewise, the steward leader must understand the urgency of his or her management responsibilities. There will be a completion.

The "harvest time" also meant there is (3) **a time of condemnation.** For the unfaithful workers in the vineyard, there was a time of reckoning. They would have to give an account of their lives, and their living, to the owner. The steward leader who has been born into God's kingdom through faith in the Lord Jesus Christ, and who walks by faith in the power of His Holy Spirit, doesn't have to worry about final condemnation. "There is now no condemnation for those who are in Christ Jesus, because through Christ Jesus the law of the Spirit of life set me free from the law of sin and death" (Rom. 8:1-2).

All believers, however, will stand before the judgment seat of Christ to give an account of their work on earth. "We will all stand before God's judgment seat. It is written: '"As surely as I live," says the Lord, "every knee will bow before me; every tongue will confess to God."' So then, each one of us will give an account of himself to God" (Rom. 14:10-12).

So a steward leader will want to be faithful in managing God's resources of time, talent, and treasure. There's a classic story of a young man who was spotted walking up and down a shoreline that was lined with starfish. The tide had brought the starfish in, and when the tide went out, the starfish lay on the beach stranded and left for dead. He was throwing some back into the ocean.

An older man who had spotted him while he walked along the beach, stopped and spoke to the young man, "Look at all those starfish! There are literally thousands of them! Do you really think you can make a difference for all of these?"

The young man stooped over, gently picked up another starfish, and threw it back into the ocean.

Then he said, "I made a difference for that one!"

Often we think our work won't make a difference in the kingdom of God. There is so much to be done, "How can we really make an impact?"

The fact is, every single act of faithfulness to the call of God on our lives will make a difference—for time and for eternity.

Developing an Annual Stewardship Plan

Suppose one of you wants to build a tower. Will he not first sit down and estimate the cost to see if he has enough money to complete it? (Luke 14:28).

>~~~<

"Generous giving is the result of an inspired motive."

—V. H. Lewis

PERHAPS YOU'VE HEARD ABOUT THE POLICEMAN that pulled over a carload of women. The policeman walked up to the car and politely said, "Ma'am, this is a 65-mph highway—why are you going so slow?"

She quickly responded, "Sir, I saw a sign that said 22, not 65!"

The policeman laughingly said, "Oh, that's not the speed limit, that's the name of the highway you're on!"

To which the lady said, "Oh! Silly me! Thanks for letting me know. I'll be more careful."

The policemen then looked in the backseat and saw two other women shaking and trembling. Tenderly the policeman said to the lady, "Excuse me, but, what's wrong with your friends back there? They're shaking something terrible."

"Oh, we just got off Highway 121," the lady responded.

Mustering up the nerve to develop an annual stewardship plan can be an unnerving experience for most church leaders! But a plan in place is better and far less nerve-racking than having no plan at all!

John Wesley had a stewardship plan. "Make all you can, save all you can, give all you can!" Obviously, he wasn't intent on reinventing the financial wheel. He would hardly be known as a simple man, however. Multiplied thousands stood in the heat of a sun-drenched field to hear him preach his eloquent sermons during his itinerant gospel mission that spanned over 100,000 miles by horseback.

As a child, he read the Scriptures in their original language. In his adult years, he laid the organizational gridwork for the greatest social reforms known to man. In old age he was sought out for his sage advice and sanctified spirit. In death, he acknowledged the presence of the divine in his hushed room.

But the utter simplicity of his stewardship plan bridges all cultural, spiritual, and generational chasms. It was a God-inspired mixture of industry, frugality, and generosity that makes perfect sense, even in an age of debit card payments on candy bars.

Understanding the Importance of an Annual Stewardship Plan

What do we mean by an annual plan? A stewardship campaign is an organized program (plan) to educate and motivate the people in the local church to spiritual faithfulness. Although finances are usually the focus, an effective stewardship campaign is not just limited to finances. It includes the broader purpose of educating people in the proper management of their time, talent, and treasure for the glory of God—the total stewardship of the believer.

During the campaign, attention is focused on biblical stewardship through various teaching methods, including Sunday School lessons, small-group Bible studies, preaching, direct mail, drama, testimonials, displays, and so forth. Usually a stewardship theme is chosen, such as "God Is Able" or "Tithing Is Christian," and the financial direction of the church is outlined in an approved budget that is presented to the whole congregation. The intent of the campaign is to make every person in the church aware of his or her responsibility to God, and to be obedient in giving through the church.

Stewardship campaigns are biblical. Just as a church has a campaign for soul winning, growth in attendance, or foreign missions, so a church ought to emphasize stewardship during a designated time of the year. A guiding principle is, whatever God has commanded His people to do, the pastor and church ought to motivate the congregation to perform.

Many mistakenly think that stewardship is just fund-raising. They often think that a stewardship program in a local church is raising money, much as a community agency raises money. Although money is raised during the campaign for the church budget, that is not the bottom line. Stewardship is not talking people out of their money. It is teaching people how to use their money properly.

Good Steward, Bad Steward

In Bible times, a steward was usually a servant who managed the household (or farm) for its owner. Jesus taught the importance of being a good steward:

Jesus told his disciples: "There was a rich man whose manager was accused of wasting his possessions. So he called him in and asked him, 'What is this I hear about you? Give an account of your management, because you cannot be manager any longer.'

"The manager said to himself, 'What shall I do now? My master is taking away my job. I'm not strong enough to dig, and I'm ashamed to beg—I know what I'll do so that, when I lose my job here, people will welcome me into their houses.'

"So he called in each one of his master's debtors. He asked the first, 'How much do you owe my master?'

"'Eight hundred gallons of olive oil,' he replied.

"The manager told him, 'Take your bill, sit down quickly, and make it four hundred.'

"Then he asked the second, 'And how much do you owe?'

"'A thousand bushels of wheat,' he replied.

"He told him, 'Take your bill and make it eight hundred.'

"The master commended the dishonest manager because he had acted shrewdly. For the people of this world are more shrewd in dealing with their own kind than are the people of the light. I tell you, use worldly wealth to gain friends for yourselves, so that when it is gone, you will be welcomed into eternal dwellings.

"Whoever can be trusted with very little can also be trusted with much, and whoever is dishonest with very little will also be dishonest with much. So if you have not been trustworthy in handling worldly wealth, who will trust you with true riches? And if you have not been trustworthy with someone else's property, who will give you property of your own?

"No servant can serve two masters. Either he will hate the one and love the other, or he will be devoted to the one and despise the other. You cannot serve both God and Money" (*Luke 16:1-13*).

Jesus used the illustration of good stewards and bad stewards to teach how we should be stewards for Him. A stewardship campaign is not to acquire money for the church but to teach believers how to live the abundant life. When Christians obey the financial principles of the Bible, their lives will be lived more abundantly, and God's work will be financed.

Why a Stewardship Campaign?

1. To help strengthen Christians. The purpose of a stewardship campaign is to strengthen every believer in the local church. Everyone, from little children who should be taught how to handle allowance money to retirees living on a fixed income, should be taught how to manage God's resources.

Stewardship emphasizes that all money belongs to God. If we realize we do not own our money, it is easier to give it back to God. For example, if we drive a company car, we know that it is not our car but is to be used for business. God wants us to treat our possessions with that attitude. God is letting us use the money He gives to us for His business. A Christian's business is God's business. Just as a company gives a salesperson rules and limits on how the company car is to be used, God has instructed us on how to use our time, talent, and treasures. Therefore, a stewardship campaign should educate church members about how to manage God's resources.

A Christian is called to be a disciple, which means to live a disciplined life. Because stewardship is management, or discipleship, it is an expression of the Christian life. Stewardship does not involve just money. It involves something deeper. It involves a discipleship to Jesus Christ that can be expressed in the way we use our money.

2. To help all Christians become obedient. During the stewardship campaign, every person in the congregation should receive campaign information and materials, because some marginal members will not attend church to hear the stewardship sermons, stewardship lessons, or see the stewardship displays. Why should they be informed? Because the campaign is not just to acquire money but to help everyone to obey God and to become stewards of His possessions.

A Christian cannot grow spiritually without being obedient. If conducted properly, more people will learn to obey the Lord Jesus Christ through the church's stewardship campaign.

3. To build relationships with marginal attenders. During a stewardship campaign, every parishioner is usually contacted. An inactive parishioner once complained, "The only time you contact me is during a stewardship campaign!" Although the campaign workers should do more than talk about money, the man complaining should be grateful that someone was concerned about his spirituality. In a stewardship campaign, those who need to become faithful are encouraged to do so through their contact with faithful workers.

4. To share our blessings. God only asks for stewardship after He has given to us. The psalmist recognized the source of all his benefits and responded, "I praise you because I am fearfully and wonderfully made; your works are wonderful, I know that full well" (139:14).

When Christians see how much God has given to them, it is embarrassing to see how little they return to Him. Good stewards manage their resources for their master's best interest.

5. To reveal our hearts. The problem with possessions is that they possess us, rather than our possessing them. A stewardship campaign reveals the hearts of all the members because they are brought to the place where they must account for the way God has blessed them during the past year. It is a time of self-evaluation, commitment to God, and potentially a time for revival.

6. To give to God. Like any investment-oriented businessperson, God expects a good return on His resources. He has placed Christians in control of His business (i.e., His ministry in the world). Surveying the parables of Jesus, it is significant that whenever the master went on a long journey, he always came back looking for a return from his farm. In application, God created us in His image and likeness. He has given us a good mind, strong wills, and the opportunities to make something of our lives for His glory. God now comes and wants us to be accountable for our gifts and abilities.

During a stewardship campaign, all Christians should be reminded that they should return finances to God so that the work of God may prosper.

7. **To teach judgment.** Christians should know that they will be judged, and that judgment is based on their stewardship. In Jesus' parables on this subject, the landowners judged their managers based on their faithfulness. Because the owner delegated the vineyard to workers does not mean they owned it. Even though the workers might develop an emotional attachment to the vines and the vineyard, the farm still did not belong to them. Yet the workers always treated the farm as if it were their own. The issue is always ownership. Who owned the vineyard?

During the stewardship campaign, Christians need to be reminded of "who owns the vineyard." That means they are reminded of who owns their houses, their bodies, and their investment portfolios. If God is the owner of all things, and He allows Christians to manage them for His glory, then a judgment day is coming.

God will judge Christians, not on the basis of what they did not have, but for what they have done with what they have been given.

There are always those who complain and say, "The church is after money." We must be careful to deal with the problem of criticism before it turns into the poison of bitterness. When a person is cut and injured, pain is associated with the wound. We never doubt the wisdom of the doctor who inflicts more pain on the already sore area by applying iodine or an antiseptic to the wound. The doctor doesn't do it to hurt needlessly but to help in the healing process. Without the medication, there would be the risk of infection. Without the teaching on stewardship, Christians risk the infection of selfishness, materialism, and worldliness.

"Now, Here's the Plan . . ."

The old adage tells us that "if we fail to plan, we plan to fail." An annual stewardship plan for the church not only helps in developing a giving church but also serves to diminish the effects of the financial downsizing that is being reflected in the offering plate these days. One financial consultant said, "Churches that initiate a planned annual stewardship program usually realize an immediate increase in giving of approximately 20 percent."

Here are 10 valuable steps for developing your stewardship plan:

Step One: Establish a Realistic Budget

Webster says a "budget" is (a) a statement of the financial position of an administration for a definite period of time based on estimates of expenditures during the period and proposals for financing them, (b) a plan for the coordination of resources and expenditures.[1]

When pastors gather, they often tell "war stories." Many of them are purple-heart veterans of the "Battle of Budget Hill." And several of them made their last stand on that battlefield. All of the wounds were not necessary, however. Wiser planning, mixed with some careful questions, common sense, good organization, and Spirit-filled speech could have turned the tides of some of those legendary battles.

One of the classic budget stories is of the elderly gentleman who saw the item "Chandelier" listed on the church's annual budget proposal. "I'm opposed to this here chandelier item," he loudly protested. "And I'm opposed to it for three very good reasons. Number one, we've gotten along for fifty years without one. Number two, nobody here knows how to play a chandelier. And number three, what we really need is one of them big lights for the vestibule!"

Obviously, that budget process lacked some things—things like communication, involvement, delegation, inventory, needs, and income. Before the budget of the United States government is ever distributed, for example, endless hours of discussion, consideration, and projections have been considered. On the other hand, some church budgets are thrown together so fast before the annual meeting that the ushers get ink on their fingers when they pass it out! Good budgeting takes careful planning.

The pastor of one large church says his church board spent four and one-half hours on 100 different financial issues, one as expensive as a $22,000 roof replacement and another as mundane as a $5 amount for pigeon spikes. After 15 minutes of discussion about the pigeon spikes, the pastor raised his hand. "I need to ask a question. What is a pigeon spike?" Several others nodded in agreement with the question. They made the discovery that pigeon spikes are something you put on the church overhangs and entryways to keep the pigeons from lighting and making a mess on the property.

The pastor reached into his pocket and pulled out $5, "I'll tell you what. I've got $5 right here. I'll give the $5 because I think this is a worthy project." One board member spoke up, "You can't do that." "Why?" the pastor asked. The response was, "We have to discuss it." The pigeon spike issue was discussed for 15 more minutes, and after 30 minutes, it was voted down.

On another issue, in 30 seconds, without a financial report, and without the money in hand to complete the project, the board approved a $22,000 roof replacement. It took 30 minutes to turn down a project that seemed practical, useful, and needed. It took only 30 seconds to approve another project that involved a great deal of money.

Church Budgeting Tips

▷ *Build your church budget with your vision plan in mind.* Always give your congregation compelling reasons for giving. Vision must be at the forefront of all invitations to give or in requests for specific budgetary matters.

▷ *Make sure your budget reflects your ministry priorities.* Avoid lumping everything into one circle and saying, "This is the way we prioritize everything." Break it down into the ministry areas of the church. There are at least five: *Stewardship and Administration, Building and Properties, Education and Equipping, Evangelism and Outreach, and Worship and Planning.* Everything that is done in the church should reflect the ministry areas.

In a *Clergy Journal* (February 1991, 9) article, Ashley Hale makes a distinction between secular fund-raising and church stewardship programs:

> ▷ Secular institutions focus on what they need to receive. The church focuses on what its members should give.

> ▷ The goal of secular organizations is bringing in funds. The church's goal is to turn people into good givers.

> ▷ Secular organizations base their appeal on duty or generosity. The church emphasizes an opportunity for spiritual development.

> ▷ Secular giving occurs on an annual cycle. The church giving cycle is weekly.

> ▷ Secular fund-raising is done through large campaigns. Church appeals are more personal.

▷ *Build a cash reserve equal to an average of one month of church income into your budget.* For example, congregations in the northern climate have discovered that there will be months like January where there will be sleet, snow, and yes, no service. The panic sets in and the church treasurer is taking hot baths and cold showers worrying about the finances.

The stress level can be reduced by simply building a cash reserve into the budget. With that achievement comes better stewardship and a better use of the gifts of God's people.

▷ *Build your church budget based on last year's usable income.* Certainly that's not the most enjoyable endeavor, but after years of overly optimistic budgeting, you'll reach the point where you will say, "We can't do this any longer. It's driving us crazy! We're stressed out."

It's far better, and easier on the nerves, to build a budget based on last year's usable income. You may say, "What do you mean, 'usable income'?" For example, usable income is not funds spent on the ski trip by the youth group. Those dollars can't be averaged into the budget—you can't expect to spend

---

Financial Update

Annual Operating Budget (Jan. 1—Dec. 31):
$684,767

Annual Need as of Oct. 13	$ 539,929
Received as of Oct. 13	519,827
BALANCE	$ -20,102
Monthly Need	$ 57,064
Received as of Oct. 13	26,854
BALANCE	$ -30,210

World Mission Budget (5/96—4/97)
Not part of operating budget

Annual Budget	$ 50,661
Received as of Oct. 13	10,356
BALANCE	$ 40,305

OPEN DOOR Campaign

36-Month Pledge Total (156 weeks)	$1,032,089
Income as of Week 53 (Oct. 13)	328,066
BALANCE	$ 704,023

that because that's not usable in the sense of spending it for the operation of the local church.

The day you begin to realize that you can base the budget on what you actually had last year to spend is the day you will begin to get real victory in the operation of the church finances.

▷ *Monitor your actual budget performance monthly.* When your finance team gets together, they begin to talk about the income. They really need to take a serious look, not only at how the finances have come in but also at how the church has operated during a given month.

▷ *Provide monthly financial statements to your church board.* Usually, if the church board is well-informed, they will be helpful. There's no need to be the Lone Ranger. There will be times when you won't want the treasurer to read the financial report aloud! But the church board needs to share in the pain. It's part of their responsibility. And it's something the church leader needs to share with them.

▷ *Seek church approval (by board or congregation) for nonbudget expenditures.* The ministry action team must be able to make budgeted expenditures, but if there's something that comes up that has not been budgeted, that item needs to be brought back to the board if the board is to operate in a realistic manner.

▷ *Never spend more than one-twelfth of your given budget without special approval.* The ministry action team may be empowered to make budgeted expenditures, but if in any month they're going to spend more than one-twelfth—with the exception of fixed expenses, like utilities and maintenance items that have been factored in—it has to be approved.

There is merit in having an empowered budget. Most of the time, ministry action teams can be trusted to make budgeted expenditures without bankrupting the church. William Easum says in his book *Making Gourmet Burgers out of Sacred Cows* that most churches worship at the sacred cow shrine of control. And, most of the time, that shrine is in the area of finances. Much of the time spent in board meeting discussions is spent on finances. An empowered budget saves discussion time. The pastor may simply say to the ministry action team, "Here's your budget. Don't spend more than one-twelfth of the given amount without permission. If you spend it, obviously, it's gone. You're finished." It will usually take only one isolated incident to convince the rest of the team that's the way it works. Enforcement is the key to making an empowered budget work.

▷ *Give regular written reports.* The question is asked, "Do you give them the details, item by item?" No. That's not what they're looking for. They're looking for a report in summary fashion of how their dollars were spent. In order to have integrity, and in order to get people on board so that they can trust the leadership, the leadership is going to have to do more accounting—letting the congregation know how their dollars are being spent.

▷ *Celebrate by spending excess income on preapproved capital budget items or projects.* The "party" shouldn't be planned until the financial status is determined. If all year long the spending is in line with the budget, if the budget is realistic, if the budget is based on last year's useable income, then most likely, there will be surplus dollars to spend at the end of the year.

When building your budget, you may also want to build a capital stewardship budget alongside that says, "We will do the following things (listed in priority) so that when we come to the end of the year, any excess will be spent on capital stewardship budget items that have been preapproved."

Certainly, there will be emergency situations that will blow your budget apart like a candlelight dinner in a dynamite factory, but your church or organization should not be caught off guard by poor planing. Wise stewardship involves "sitting down and counting the cost" to see if "there is enough money."

Good budgeting will also help to prevent the public relations nightmares of unpaid bills to community vendors and suppliers. The story is told of a customer who fell behind in his payments. When questioned by the store where he owed money, the customer begged for some time so that he could pay off a debt he owed to his mother. The store manager replied, "Sir, our records show we've done more for you than your mother ever did. She only carried you 9 months and we've carried you 15!"

Step Two: Appeal to the Six Pockets of Giving

In every church there are at least six pockets of giving, and there are people who have dollars to give to a certain cause. If you don't ask for those dollars, you'll lose them.

1. The maintenance pocket. The givers to this pocket are the general operation givers. They are people who are just going to give to the general fund. They are concerned with paying the utilities, salaries, supplies, and general maintenance. They tithe and that's it—nothing else.

2. The missions pocket. When you've said "World Missions" to them, you've said it all. When it comes to raising dollars for overseas ministries, you can always count on them being on board. Certain members want most of their money to go to foreign missions, and often want at least some of that money to go to outreach, usually out of the concern for the Great Commission.

3. The benevolence pocket. This is the "cup of cold water" person. The person who is always interested in helping the homeless or the hungry. One church has a group that receives an offering every Wednesday night just to help take care of the homeless in their community, and they are very faithful to support that cause.

4. The building pocket. Their cause is brick and mortar. They're the first to offer a "challenge gift" when raising funds for the new family life center. They propose the paving of the parking lot. They want the facilities expanded. They're the volunteer members of the committee on building the new family life center.

5. The education pocket. Because some church members value higher education, they direct their money to the denomination's Bible college or liberal arts college. Receive an offering for the college's new science hall or library, and they are all ears!

6. The evangelism pocket. There are individuals who have a desire to see the world come to know Christ, and when you say, "Let's evangelize the world," they'll be right there to help you in the process.

You may also want to seek the permission of your church board to focus on those pockets in a giving emphasis at least twice each year. For example, you may want to ask your congregation to help with a missions project apart from the denomination's missions offering emphasis. You could receive a Sunday evening offering for a missionary that has a special need, or give a love offering for a missionary couple visiting on deputation work. You'll be surprised at how they'll respond to a special missions project above and beyond their tithe. The interest is there, and the dollars are there to support that interest.

"Pocket" Principles

1. If the church doesn't appeal to these pockets of giving in their stewardship plan, if the church doesn't ask for their dollars, someone else will. Media ministries will. Missions organizations

will. Educational institutions will. Relief organizations will. So you will want to have a concentrated plan to include those giving pockets in your stewardship plan during the year.

2. Money in one pocket usually will not go for projects of another pocket. The emotional or spiritual commitment of members usually does not transfer from one project to another.

3. Finances that are not given to the local church will usually go to an interdenominational or humanitarian agency. Postponing a capital fund project usually means the church is losing money it could otherwise use.

4. Church leaders are not aware of what parishioners have in their pockets until they are presented with a financial challenge. People give in response to a challenge, and their preference is unknown until they give.

5. Once parishioners' pockets are opened, they will give again from the same pockets with the same motivations to the same kinds of needs.

Step Three: Distribute Numbered Offering Envelopes to All Church Attenders

You'll remember that one of the goals in developing a giving church is for givers to give regularly. Tithing envelopes help make giving a regular habit and also help in keeping accurate giving records.

You'll want to make them prominent in your overall stewardship plan.

Whenever new people join the church, they need to receive a complimentary box of tithing envelopes. By doing so, you are letting the new members know that you expect them to be faithful in their financial support of the church.

Since financial credibility is so important to the local church, the numbered tithe envelopes also are a great aid in keeping accurate records. In these days of government scrutiny and regulations about nonprofit matters, it is especially important to have a proper recordkeeping system.

Step Four: Mail Quarterly Giving Statements to All Parishioners

It's said that a wealthy man died and went to heaven. On his "tour" of the celestial city, he came to a magnificent home.

"Who lives there?" the man asked.

The angel guide answered, "Well, on earth he was a gardener." That excited the rich man as he thought, "If this is what a gardener lives in, I wonder what my mansion will look like."

They came across another, even more magnificent, mansion. "Awesome!" the man said. "Who lives there?"

"She was a worker in an orphanage," the angel guide replied.

The rich man was really excited now! "Just imagine what my mansion will look like, if she has a mansion like that!" he thought.

Finally they came to a tiny eight-by-eight shack, with no windows and only a piece of cloth for a door—the most modest home in all of heaven. Reluctantly he asked, "And, who lives here?"

The angel guide held his hand out to the little bungalow, "This is your home, sir."

"I don't understand," the wealthy man responded. "Why is my home so tiny?"

The angel guide replied, "Well, sir, I'm sorry to say it, but that's all we could build with what you sent us to work with."

Two things will happen immediately when you mail giving statements:

1. You will be able to reconcile giving records. Incorrect records will be discovered, as often happens. At times, an incorrect amount is recorded by the tithing secretary due to the reversing of a number sequence, for instance. One number out of sequence could make all the difference. At other times, an incorrect amount will be noted due to the illegible handwriting of the giver. Many of the envelopes and checks are written in a hurry—some during the offertory prayer and others during the offertory song. The pressure is on to get the check in the plate while it is passed through the pew row, so some checks and offering envelope notations end up looking like prescription slips handed to the local pharmacist.

2. The next thing that probably will happen is an immediate increase in giving. Your givers will be reminded that they're not up-to-date on some of the pledges they have made. By sending them a quarterly statement, it gives them an opportunity to see where they stand, and often the next Sunday's offering will be a reflection of that revived interest.

In two-income families, for example, it's easy for one or more checks to vary from month to month, and consequently the tithing amount will vary. The busyness of those two-income families may also result in a forgotten payment on a pledge. The intent was to pay the tithes or keep the commitment on a pledge, but there was a natural oversight. Quarterly statements are a gentle way of telling givers, "You're behind on that building campaign pledge (missions pledge)" without saying, "Get with it!"

A letter from the pastor may accompany the giving statement. Here's an example.

> Dear Members and Friends of Trinity Church:
>
> Good day! I am writing to thank you for your faithful stewardship to Trinity Church of the Nazarene. Because of your regular support, our church is strong financially.
>
> You have my pledge that your church leaders will be faithful stewards of your continued financial gifts. You are a blessing to me! Thanks again for your gift this quarter.
>
> You are loved,
>
>
> Pastor Stan Toler
> Eph. 3:20-21
> Enclosure
> P.S.   If you have any questions concerning the accuracy of your giving record, please call our financial secretary, (name and phone number)   .

Step Five: Never "Take" the Offering; Rather, "Receive" the Offering

The offering time in a worship service should be a time of celebration. Your parishioners should look *forward to it,* not *down on it!*

In one church, a great fall attendance campaign was in gear. A western "roundup" theme highlighted the campaign, so everybody was wearing western wear. The ushers were dressed in western shirts, pants, vests, and cowboy boots. All of a sudden one of the ushers had the idea to put a western-style kerchief over his face and march to the front of the church with a double-barrel shotgun in hand. When he got to the front of the church, he faced the audience and announced, "Now, we want you all to give generously this morning!"

"Taking" the offering often feels like that to your parishioners. It almost makes them feel like the ushers will be toting shotguns. It sounds as if someone is making them do something they don't want to do.

"There are still two collection plates out there somewhere."
© Steve Phelps. Used by permission.

"Receiving" the offering makes for a greater time of celebration and worship. Here are some suggestions for making the offering time a "precious moment" rather than a precarious moment:

▷ *Use drama to illustrate the need for giving.* Use a brief skit, for example, that communicates the importance of giving God His portion. You may also want to include some young people who have the ability to dramatize in an effective way. By so doing, you not only communicate to the audience but also give the young person involved a hands-on learning experience.

▷ *Use humor to reduce tension about giving.* A brief story that "packs powerful truth" into a "powerful punch line" will put your audience at ease and help them understand that giving is a celebration rather than a dour duty.

▷ *Use a giving witness to share briefly.* In an age of "infomercials," your people will understand the importance of first-person accounts. Prearrange to have someone share what God has done through his or her giving, and how He has poured blessings into his or her life that overflow. One church asks a different layperson each week to give a brief (one to three minute) testimony. A brief biography about the person is placed in the bulletin, the designated layperson receives some simple guidelines by mail for presenting his or her testimony.

▷ *Use Scripture for a moment of meditation.* Before the offering is received, share a classic portion of God's Word like Luke 6:38, "Give, and it will be given to you. A good measure, pressed down, shaken together and running over, will be poured into your lap. For with the measure you use, it will be measured to you." A "brief" comment and application of that verse could be the very thing that will strike a chord of response in a potential giver's heart. God promises that His Word "will not return unto me empty, but will accomplish what I desire and achieve the purpose for which I sent it" (Isa. 55:11).

▷ *Use stories that will support your mission.* For example, share some story that will illustrate the need for missions support, by relating some communication from the mission field. Show your parishioners how God has used their giving to bless a work or a worker overseas.

▷ *Be sure to give your offering first.* The shepherd is called to be "an example to the flock." And you can be sure that the flock will take notice when the shepherd places an offering envelope in the offering plate before the offering is received.

One pastor had just finished a series of stewardship messages. One Sunday morning, a parishioner asked to speak to the congregation. Knowing the witness and spiritual influence of the man, the pastor agreed.

He began, "Pastor, I'd like to testify to how good God's been. My wife and I have practiced the principles of stewardship that you've been preaching about. If there are any of you young folk here who would just try this tithing thing for 90 days, we will refund your money if you don't find this to be a wonderful way of celebrating the goodness of God."

Several years later, the pastor referred to that incident and looked to the couple in the worship service, "Do we still have your guarantee?" The couple responded with enthusiasm, "Yes, pastor, you still have our guarantee!" Giving is a celebration of the goodness of our God, and that should be communicated to the congregation during the implementation of your stewardship plan.

Step Six: Teach Children the Importance of Giving

Your stewardship plan must have an emphasis for children. They must be taught from the beginning the privilege of giving. For many, the first experience in giving probably happened in Sunday School. Maybe it was during the "opening exercises" (when there was very little exercise). During the "penny march," the littlest children learn the joy of giving to God. Many times the accompaniment song wasn't too inspiring, but the joy of marching to the front of the sanctuary and tossing those copper coins into a bucket was contagious.

The pastor may want to include an illustrated message especially for children on the importance of Christian giving during the stewardship month. Children can even be given their own box of offering envelopes upon request. It will teach them about their responsibility and teach them habits of regular giving.

This is seen in the story of a little girl, the daughter of the church treasurer, who brought an offering envelope to her Sunday School teacher. On the front of the envelope she had written in the space for the name, "Jesus." The amount was 25 cents, so she was giving her tithe. As she handed it to her Sunday School teacher she asked, "I want to know if you can get this directly to Jesus for me?" Obviously, she was bypassing the church treasurer (her father) and going directly to the source.

It would be wonderful if we could get all of our children to understand the importance of giving their offering to Jesus. It will help if we include them in all of our building campaign offerings, world mission offerings, world evangelization offerings, and so forth. Let them be a part of the process. Let them come in and share with the congregation en masse, a gift to the building program, for instance.

Step Seven: Never Ask for Money at Events That Have Been Designed to Reach the Unchurched

As a rule of thumb, churches ought to have at least four events per year designed to evangelize unchurched persons. At those events, an offering should not be received. Those events can be covered in the budget plan or funded by an offering in a previous service. You can explain that the funds are being raised in advance to offset the cost of the event and will help to diminish the complaints by the unchurched that the church is always asking for money.

In fact, by eliminating the time taken for an offering in those events, there is more time to share a simple plan of salvation or ask for interest in upcoming events by way of the church publications. It's amazing the look on the faces of your visitors when you announce, "Our ushers are going to come. They're going to receive your response card in the offering plate, but we will not be accepting money tonight."

Step Eight: Overcome the Fear of Preaching About Money by Planning Annual Stewardship Messages on the Subject of Giving

Robert Russell said, "The reason I wasn't preaching on stewardship was cowardly. I wanted to please people more than I wanted to please God."

Many times preachers can't preach on stewardship because their own "tithing house" is not in order. Pastors cannot ask people to give one dollar if they don't give a dollar. Equal giving is not the question; it's equal sacrifice—and pastors are not exempt. Pastors, first and foremost, must be tithers. Period.

Church treasurers and finance committee members must also have their "tithing house" in order. If you collect and count the money, and you don't tithe, then a time of repentance is in order. Maybe you have strong debt. Maybe you're like the man whose wife entered the fellowship hall during a church supper and his friend commented, "My, your wife just looks electrifying tonight!" The husband replied, "She ought to look electrifying, everything she has on is charged."

Maybe you have all sorts of circumstances that would keep you from tithing. But "God does windows" and He will honor your obedience to His Word in the paying of your tithe. He will "pour out a blessing" for those who will obey Him in their giving. If that principle isn't practiced among the church leadership, then it can't be expected among the rest of the congregation.

You may ask, "What do I preach?"

You might start with the "Macedonian Model of Giving" (2 Cor. 8:1-9).

1. The Macedonians gave willingly.
2. The Macedonians gave beyond their ability.
3. The Macedonians gave enthusiastically.
4. The Macedonians gave God their best.

There probably will be three responses to your stewardship message. First, be prepared for those who give no matter what you do. There's a group of people in your church that you can just count on.

Second, there are those who will never give, no matter what you do.

Third, there will be those who will respond and start tithing. They may come from a new target group.

Reaching Target Groups

Let's look more closely at some target groups for expanding your tithing base.

Guest attenders is a target group. You probably won't want to ask them for money immediately. But they are prospective givers. Most of the people who attend Sunday School on a regular basis have some insight about giving, but many times, because more guests attend worship services, they are potentially a greater source for expansion.

Occasional attenders is another target group. Church leaders are wise to keep the communication channels open. One well-known pastor once made the statement that there is no way you can get off his mailing list once you're on it—not even if you die! Letters to those who attend your church sporadically can be a channel of communicating financial needs. And those very letters could be the link that ties them more securely to the church fellowship.

Your **faithful members** form another target group. George Gallup, at an NAE Convention, said, "Fifty percent of the people in your church aren't going to be involved in any way, shape or form, no matter what you do or ask them to do." He added, "Ten percent are doing the work of the ministry in most local churches. If you narrow it down, you'll also find that the bulk of the income in your church—sometimes up to one half of the dollars given—come right out of the church leadership. Why? You've captured their imagination; you've gotten them involved."

Lay ministry must increase. People need to move from the stands to the playing field. Your stewardship plan must have a place for that commitment to ministry. Again, Gallup says, "Forty percent are just waiting to be asked, and they would be willing to say 'Yes!' if you ask them." Similarly, if you could get 50 percent of the congregation to give on regular basis, church income would increase.

Step Nine: Plan a Stewardship Month

You'll find that an entire month of stewardship emphasis will help you in developing a giving church.

Calendarizing is crucial. When should you conduct stewardship month? January is often suggested as one of the most effective times to conduct a stewardship emphasis. The New Year is often a time when people are making spiritual resolutions, and the resolution to regularly and systematically give to the church would be a good one! Also, January is often one of the financial "slack times," and so an emphasis on giving is advantageous.

If that month isn't the best for your church, you can choose any month. D. L. Moody was once approached, "Mr. Moody, I don't like your soul-winning plan."

Mr. Moody said, "And what plan do you use?"

The man replied, "Well, I haven't found one I like."

Moody responded, "Well, I like my way of doing it better than your way of not doing it."

In cooperation with your finance committee or church board, determine what month is best suited for your stewardship emphasis, and begin to form a calendar of events.

There are seven key ingredients involved in planning a stewardship month emphasis:

1. Appoint a team leader. The team leader must be someone who is committed to the Lord Jesus Christ, who can effectively recruit and train others, and is well-known as a regular tither/giver in the church.

2. Form a ministry action team. The team may include your finance committee, or it may be a committee appointed specifically for the stewardship month. Team members may include someone who will lead a prayer emphasis for the campaign, someone who is adept at public relations, someone who likes to make personal contacts or telephone contacts, and so forth.

3. Select a theme. The theme should reflect your vision plan for the church, should be memorable, should reflect your ministry priorities, and should be biblical.

4. Send out weekly letters. The congregation needs to hear regularly from the ministry action team. The letters should not come from the pastor. Laypersons sign them and volunteers send them out. The first three letters should talk about the planned stewardship message and the emphasis should be on the stewardship of life—not money. (In fact, a "P.S." can be added to reemphasize that the pastor's stewardship message will not be on money.)

5. Preach a series of messages on the stewardship of life. (See Appendix.)

6. Communicate the vision. On the first Sunday of the stewardship month, you may want to reflect on the mission statement of the church. An application is made of the mission statement about how it relates to everyday life. Parishioners should be challenged to develop a personal mission statement and vision statement if they relate to the church's statement.

7. Distribute the budget that was designed by the finance ministry action team and approved by the church board on the Sunday you speak about giving. The stewardship of life certainly includes giving. On the Sunday you emphasize giving, you'll want to make the church budget available to your congregation.

Of the four messages on the stewardship of life, the first three should seldom mention money. One pastor says he doesn't mention money all year long except for the one Sunday of his stewardship month—usually the very last Sunday.

On the fourth Sunday—the money Sunday—the emphasis should be a thoroughly biblical, uncompromising, and practical message on the responsibility of Christian giving.

In preparation for that sermon, you may want to announce that the budget will be distributed on that Sunday to let the congregation know how the church board and the ministry team will be spending the money throughout the year. You may also want to let them know that there will be an accounting of how well the money was spent last year.

So, the fourth letter mailed to the congregation will say, "Pastor will be preaching on money. He will talk about giving. And

CREATE A RESPONSE FORM FOR COMMITMENT SUNDAY

"Partnership with God" (Sample)

D. L. Moody said, "If God is your partner, make your plans big."
Realizing God's desire to enter a covenant relationship with me; and
Realizing without Him I can do nothing of eternal significance; and
Realizing that my obedience to Him is the key to this relationship:

My response—
My commitment to tithe is based upon the following truths:
1. God owns everything.
2. God expects me to tithe.
3. God promises to meet the needs of a faithful steward.

Therefore, I commit the first 10 percent of my income to the Lord through my local church.

☐ I will begin tithing.   ☐ I already tithe.

Name _____

City, State, Zip _____

Giving Number _____   ☐ I need giving envelopes.

Stewardship Development Ministries

there also will be a report from the finance ministry action team on how we spent your dollars."

"Money Sunday" could be one of the best-attended Sundays of the entire year—especially if you add in your announcement, "You probably won't want to come. You probably won't want to be a part of this, but I'm going to do it, and it's going to be red hot, and by the way, we will tell you how we spent your money. And we'll also tell you how we're going to spend your money next year."

Don't be afraid to ask for a commitment to give regularly. When you come to the conclusion of the message on giving, ask your congregation to bow their heads in a moment of meditation, and pray, asking God to guide them in their giving habits. Be sure to ask them to analyze their lifestyles and their checkbooks. Encourage them to form a partnership with God.

The pastor may then say, "In a moment, I'm going to ask you to make a check mark by the place where it says that you are already tithing or that you will begin to tithe. With that in mind, I want you to take another moment to examine your heart and see if you've been faithful all year long. If you haven't, ask God to forgive you. If you have, mark the box that says you will keep tithing. If you haven't tithed at all, and God is speaking to you through this message today, I want you to mark the box that says you will begin tithing."

Some may be uncomfortable with that process. The pastor may offer the alternative of putting that form in their Bible or the spiritual journal that they carry to church. They also may be encouraged to look at the form from time to time just to see if they are up to date.

Often, there will be checks in the offering plate the very next week that will reflect the decisions new tithers have made. The pastor has simply asked them to sign a partnership with God.

Step Ten: Build a Stewardship Planning Calendar

Every church needs a plan of action for stewardship development. Be sure to designate a stewardship month emphasis.

Further, in developing an annual stewardship plan, be sure to:

▷ Emphasize giving as an act of worship.

▷ Inform your congregation of significant offering achievements.

▷ Offer workshops on money management and financial planning.

▷ Praise your congregation for their faithfulness in giving. Always celebrate the generosity of God's people.

Your stewardship plan should involve lots of praise. Your congregation should be recognized for their faithfulness in giving. You'll want to say "Thank you!" over and over again, write them notes, send them updates, praise them in your church publications. Always celebrate the generosity of your people.

5 SUPPORTING THE PASTORAL TEAM

Now we ask you, brothers, to respect those who work hard among you, who are over you in the Lord and who admonish you (1 Thess. 5:12).

><><

"We cannot serve God and mammon; but we can serve God with mammon."
—Robert E. Speer

THERE'S A CLASSIC STORY ABOUT A NEW PASTOR who went to an auto dealer for a new car. He was pleasantly surprised to find out that the dealer had attended his worship service. After a look through the car lot, he spotted a car that caught his eye. Looking closer, he discovered it had all the desired options. The sticker price wasn't as appealing, however. Announcing his choice to the dealer, he tried to explain that the car was just what he wanted but the price was a little too steep, "Need I remind you that I'm just a poor preacher." The dealer replied, "No, you don't have to remind me, I heard you preach last Sunday!"

Whether or not the preacher's sermon scores a "10" on a given Sunday has nothing to do with his or her right to be supported financially. The fact is, if most congregations paid their pastoral team an hourly wage, they could not afford them. For example, the pastoral team is to be "on call" 24 hours per day, seven days a week, if necessary, to care for the spiritual, emotional, financial, and relational needs of the congregation. A salary agreement that is fair, reasonable, and agreeable to all "interested parties" is an act of wise stewardship on the congregation's part and also on the part of the pastoral team.

YOU MIGHT BE A PREACHER IF . . .

You drive a Buick with over 100,000 miles on it.

Stan Toler and Mark Toler-Hollingsworth, *You Might Be a Preacher If . . .* , vol. 1 (Tulsa, Okla.: Albury Publishing, 1995). Illustration by Cory Edwards. Used with permission.

Making Ministry Ends Meet

A recent Gallup survey indicated that among professionals, the clergy was listed second only to pharmacists in their "honesty and ethical standards." But, Gary McIntosh says the clergy continues to be one of the most underpaid professions. Clergypersons ranked seventh among the 10 "worst paying jobs requiring degrees."

The authors' view is that churches really need to elevate the pay level of their pastors.

Perhaps you've heard the story of the preacher who took a shortcut through the appliance section of a department store. A

salesman stopped him and said, "Excuse me, sir, would you be interested in one of the freezers we have on sale?"

"No, thank you," the preacher replied, "I'm afraid that won't fit our budget."

"But, sir," the salesman interrupted, "you'll save enough on your food bill to pay for it!"

"Maybe so," answered the preacher, "but right now we're making payments for a motorcycle on the auto expense money we saved, and payments for the air conditioner on the electric bill we saved, and payments for the house on the rent we saved.

"Frankly, my friend," the preacher said, "right now we have so many payments, we can't afford to save any more money!"

How Pastors Feel About Their Pay*

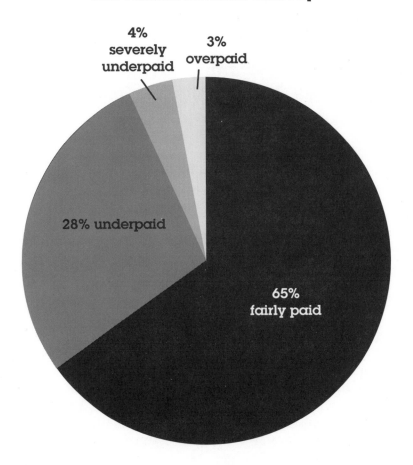

*John C. LaRue Jr., "Pastors and Salary Satisfaction," *Your Church* (May/June 1998), 88.

The pastor's pay is often discussed with as much frequency as the weather forecast. Its ups and downs, intentions and exceptions, "appreciations" and depreciations are flames that have burned the "midnight oils" in many church financial meetings.

And there is often a great misunderstanding about what the pastoral team actually receives. That's evidenced in the story of the sons of a lawyer, a doctor, and a minister. During a discussion one day, the lawyer's son bragged, "My dad goes to court and makes $2,000 in fees—in one day!"

"That's nothing!" the doctor's son responded. "My dad goes to the operating room, performs one surgical procedure, and makes $3,000!"

"Oh, spare me!" the minister's son chimed in. "My dad goes to church, talks for 15 minutes, and it takes four men to carry his salary out!"

><><

"For the Scripture says, 'Do not muzzle the ox while it is treading out the grain,' and 'The worker deserves his wages.'"

(1 Tim. 5:18)

Why Should the Pastoral Team Be Paid?

One of the first questions asked by the church's salary evaluation committee is, "Why should the pastor receive a salary at all?"

Or they may say, "Others in this church give many hours of service and don't get paid for it!"

Or, "After all, we didn't call the pastor into ministry, God did!"

To put things in perspective, consider what America spends in one day, according to an article published by Lincoln Benefits Company of Nebraska: $2.5 million washing cars, $40 million on auto repairs caused by rust, $10 million for pornography, $8,000 per second on entertainment and recreation, $300 million on clothes, $125,000 for Elvis Presley merchandise and tours, $5.5 million to parking meters.

Another study published in the *Chicago Tribune* reveals that

Americans spend $12 billion on candy, $2.5 billion on gum, and $19 billion on lotteries. In comparison, "The total annual budget for Protestant overseas ministries, some 600 in all, is $1.7 billion."

In light of the eternal, moneys invested in people responsible for the care and feeding of souls is money well spent.

The basis for a financial support of the ministry is seen in these principles and precedents found in God's Word:

The ministry of Christ's disciples was supported by others. "Calling the Twelve to him, he sent them out two by two and gave them authority over evil spirits. These were his instructions: 'Take nothing for the journey except a staff—no bread, no bag, no money in your belts. Wear sandals but not an extra tunic. Whenever you enter a house, stay there until you leave that town'" (Mark 6:7-10; cf. Luke 9:3-6).

Christ specifically instructed the disciples to depend on the provisions of their host families—the local "church fellowship." Notice that the implied instructions to the supporting host family included the provision of food, finances, housing, and clothing. It could be said that the salary "package" of the early disciples was, in many ways, more inclusive than some modern salary packages.

Some church members would breathe a sigh of relief to know that it's not customary in these days to house the pastor's family in their own homes. In pioneer days, the circuit-ridin' preacher would often reside with one or more families during the ministry tenure. That practice certainly gave the preacher an opportunity for getting to know the congregation, but it probably fostered a "spiritual claustrophobia" that resulted in some pretty tense moments.

Paul praised the Philippian church for its faithfulness in supporting his ministry.

As you Philippians know, in the early days of your acquaintance with the gospel, when I set out from Macedonia, not one church shared with me in the matter of giving and receiving, except you only; for even when I was in Thessalonica, you sent me aid again and again when I was in need. Not that I am looking for a gift, but I am looking for what may be credited to your account. I have received full payment and even more; I am amply supplied, now that I have received from Epaphroditus the gifts you sent. They are a fragrant offering, an acceptable sacrifice, pleasing to God. And my God will meet all your needs according to his glorious riches in Christ Jesus (*Phil. 4:15-19; cf. 2 Cor. 9:1-11; 11:7-9*).

It should also be noted that God blessed the faithfulness of the church in supporting the ministry of the pastoral team according to

His promise, "My God will meet all your needs according to his glorious riches in Christ Jesus" (Phil. 4:19). The saints used to say, "You can't outgive God!" Both the apostle and the church understood that very well.

The man who asked his pastor if he should pay his tithe on the "gross" or the "net" of his income received the well-known response, "Well, in which way do you want God to pour out His blessings?"

Paul outlines the biblical basis for paying pastors. Again, the apostle Paul reminds the church of its financial duty to the pastor:

> Who serves as a soldier at his own expense? Who plants a vineyard and does not eat of its grapes? Who tends a flock and does not drink the milk? Do I say this merely from a human point of view? Doesn't the Law say the same thing? For it is written in the Law of Moses: "Do not muzzle an ox while it is treading out the grain." Is it about oxen that God is concerned? Surely he says this for us, doesn't he? Yes, this was written for us, because when the plowman plows and the thresher threshes, they ought to do so in the hope of sharing in the harvest. If we have sown spiritual seed among you, is it too much if we reap a material harvest from you? If others have this right of support from you, shouldn't we have it all the more? *(1 Cor. 9:7-12).*

John Wesley commented that the thresher and the plowman ought not to be disappointed, they ought to share the fruit of their labors, "And so ought they who labor in God's husbandry." We live in an age when the bonuses of most company CEOs often far exceed their salaries. But most pastors' salaries, in a lifetime of ministry, would not equal one of those CEO bonuses. Whose work is more important, the one who sows for time or the one who sows for eternity?

Paul suggests that the laborer has a right to share the material increase of the field. Most church organizations have verified that in their charter or their organizational manual. Upon issuing a call to a pastor, the local church should specify its proposed remuneration. Once the salary and benefits outlined in the agreement have been agreed upon, the church should consider their financial commitment to the pastor a morally binding agreement.

The story is told of a preacher who made an announcement to his Sunday morning congregation, "I have three sermons in my hands. The first is a $100 sermon that lasts 15 minutes. The second sermon is a $50 one, and it lasts 30 minutes. The last is a $10 sermon, and one of my favorites, I might add. It lasts an hour and a half."

The crowd looked a bit concerned, and not a few had already made their choice when the pastor announced, "In a few minutes I'll be preaching one of those sermons. But right now, we're going to receive your morning tithes and offerings, and by your response, we'll see which sermon I'll preach."

It must be remembered that a layperson's salary compares to a minister's salary and housing. The pastor's salary may be compared to the national standards of other occupations:

Determine where the pastor's job should fall:

Physician	$163,000
Airline Pilot	99,700
Computer Engineer	73,300
Computer Systems Analyst	56,000
Pharmacist	50,900
Physical Therapist	50,800
Managerial/Professional	41,132
Computer Programmer	40,000
High School Teacher	37,300
Registered Nurse	37,000
Electrical, Gas, or Sanitation Service	36,816
Special-education Teacher	35,000
Staff Psychologist	34,166
Telephone Communications	33,571
Radiological Technologist	30,400
Sales Occupations	28,288
Mechanics	28,000
Clerical	26,468
Manufacturing	25,584
Machine Operators	25,317
Farmers	14,248
Retail Workers	12,881

Data from the U.S. Bureau of Labor Statistics

The Church's Duties in Supporting the Pastoral Team

In days of old, members of the church congregation would provide the preacher with farm surplus to supplement the income. A dozen eggs or more, potatoes, corn, chickens, or even a slaughtered cow or pig would be considered compensation for someone's ministerial duties. But most department stores aren't accepting a dozen eggs for payment on furniture these days. They want cash.

Today's pastoral team lives in a culture that makes some expectations of its professionals. For example, you wouldn't feel very comfortable if your dentist walked into the treatment room dressed in dirty jeans, a torn sweatshirt, and sandals. You might say, "a dentist should look like a dentist."

Likewise, folks wouldn't feel very comfortable if the pastor showed up to do a wedding ceremony dressed in dirty jeans, a torn sweatshirt, and sandals. Horrified, they might delay the wedding until the pastor returned dressed in something more appropriate. "A pastor should dress like a pastor," they might say.

"Dressing like a pastor," however, is not cheap. Even at discount prices, professional attire involves a sizeable investment.

Or, imagine signing up for a night class at the local university's extension program and discovering that your professor not only doesn't have any letters behind her name but hasn't even finished high school.

"Excuse me," you might say to the registrar, "I'm not going to invest my time or my money in this class if the college educator has never been college educated!"

Likewise, some would say, "We want a pastor who is well-educated."

But anyone negotiating loan grants to get their Johnny or Susie through just the first year of college knows that the price of higher education is getting higher.

One financial consultant estimates that some of today's seminary graduates will be carrying a debt load in excess of $50,000. Loan payments and educational fees put a noticeable strain on the pastoral team's budget—and often an emotional strain on their lives as well.

Imagine another scenario. You would be rather curious to see a laboratory technician examining a bacteria culture by just leaning over the worktable to get the closest look possible without the aid of a microscope.

You would be especially curious if that culture was the one your HMO was paying for! "Technicians should have the proper equipment to do their jobs," you would probably say.

Likewise, the pastoral team should be equipped to minister. The price of one study Bible could be in excess of $70 in today's

Christian bookstore. Add to that the price of commentaries, study helps, magazine subscriptions, newspapers, computer hardware and software, and other media to keep the pastoral team on the cutting edge, the pastoral team has already made a sizeable investment.

The local church, through its board, has several financial commitments it can make to its pastoral team. They may include:

1. **An annual pastor salary review.** In a survey by John C. LaRue Jr. for *Your Church* magazine, it was discovered that in regard to pastoral salaries "4 of 10 churches don't have an annual plan for a raise." Of course, not all local church finances will allow a raise in salary. Extenuating circumstances may prohibit it. But in most cases, a salary review and a subsequent raise in salary or benefits could be budgeted and would be to the advantage of the church. First, it would not only raise the esteem of the pastoral team, especially in their feelings of worth, but also make the congregation feel better about its ability to support them. Second, it would also be an added incentive for the church in trusting the Lord to provide the increase.

Waldo J. Werning, in his book *Supply-Side Stewardship*, contrasts stewardship models. Some parishioners give "to" the needs of the church, while others give "from" God's blessings through the church. He says, "The 'from' approach has the biblical emphasis on

Fringe Benefits of Senior and Solo Pastors*

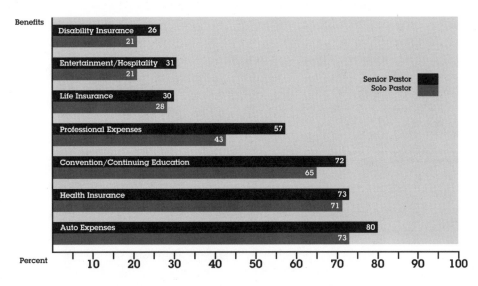

*John C. LaRue Jr., "Pastors and Fringe Benefits," *Your Church* (January/February 1998), 96.

identifying each individual's gifts and then using these gifts through the church or other mission agencies."[1] Considering that God will always supply resources for His work, as has been mentioned, the church is well advised to encourage the individual gifts of its pastoral team, God's representatives, by faithfully—and diligently—supporting their work financially.

2. Continuing educational opportunities. There's a delightful story of a traveling minister in a strange town who asked a small boy for directions to the post office. After thanking the boy, he said, "You seem to be a bright young man. How would you like to come hear me preach tonight? I'm gonna tell people how to get to heaven."

The boy responded, "You're going to tell people how to get to heaven, and you don't even know how to get to the post office?"

Paul advised Timothy to be skilled in telling people how to get to heaven, "Do your best to present yourself to God as one approved, a workman who does not need to be ashamed and who correctly handles the word of truth" (2 Tim. 2:15).

In his acceptance speech as his party's presidential candidate, George Bush told how the mothers of the Jewish ghettos in the East would pour honey on a book so the children would know that learning is sweet. Pastors who share the truth need the spiritual and educational depth to do so.

Ministers of the gospel have a greater opportunity to continue their education today than in any other time. From video training offered by denominational agencies to Internet classes offered by accredited Bible colleges and universities, there are many ways the modern pastoral team can further a ministerial education.

It's not only the pastoral team that benefits from a minister's continuing education but the church benefits as well. The pastoral team's insights and practical knowledge from Bible survey, theology, Christian education, management, business, preaching, or writing courses can be well worth the investment for a local church.

3. Skill-sharpening seminar opportunities. Tom Nesbitt, in an article for *Challenge to Evangelism Today,* says, "The first law of the spiritual life is the law of receptivity: An organism can only give what it has taken in or received:

- A flower can only bloom and give out after taking in water, sunlight, and nutrients from the soil.
- A violinist or soloist can only give a great performance after years of taking in musical training, practicing, rehearsals.
- An Olympic athlete can only give a world-class gymnastics

performance after taking in hours of sacrificial training, self-discipline, and repetitious workouts."

Pastoral team members are required to constantly give—spiritually, mentally, emotionally, and physically. It only stands to reason that those resources must be replenished. It is amazing how church staff members can take part in a grueling off-site seminar or conference and still come away refreshed! The reason is that they've been on the receiving end during that conference time and not the giving. Nearly every facet of the pastoral team member's life can be enhanced by periodic off-site training.

The local church also benefits from those times of training. Often a ministry idea is born in the minister's heart during a seminar or conference experience—even while someone else is speaking. God often inspires new ideas for local church ministry in those who are away from the "front lines." Those "precious moments" of inspiration usually happen because of the change in ministry scenery —and a fulfillment of the principle that, in the daily regimen, "we can't see the forest because of the trees."

4. Time off for rest and refreshment. To paraphrase a familiar phrase, it could be said that "Seven days without a *day off* makes one weak."

One major corporation has as one of its slogans, "You deserve a break today, go ahead and get away . . ." The pastoral team often does deserve a break! And family deserves the break as well. Hours of ministry away from home—or in locked-away study time, at required meetings, in off-site conferences and seminars—all add up to extended times of separation from a minister's loved ones.

Not only are the pastoral team's loved ones affected, but also the team member is impacted. Frayed nerves, ill health, and spiritual neglect are most often the result of intense days and weeks without a break.

One pastor said, "I never used to take my full vacation. But one day, I realized that 50 years from now, no one would really care whether I did or not." The pastor continued, "People in my congregation take their full vacation, in fact if they don't, they could be subject to the censure of their supervisors or labor representatives." He said joyfully, "I now take every single day of the vacation time allotted me. I'm happier in my ministry, my family is happier in my ministry, and the church is happier in my ministry. The reason is simple. When I come back from vacation, not only is the church's *minister* refreshed but my entire *ministry* is refreshed!"

5. Professional expense reimbursement. In a minister's memo from Don Walters, director of Pensions and Benefits for the Church of the Nazarene, ministry expenses were addressed in the following manner:

> For too long, churches and ministers have lumped together into a single concept the "cost of a minister" and the "cost of a ministry." These are actually two distinct concepts. For proper planning and church budgeting they must be kept separate.

> The "cost of ministry" includes those costs related to the work of the minister . . . they include the following business and professional expense reimbursements:

> Automobile
> Continuing Education
> Convention
> Hospitality
> Pastor's Professional Library
> Dues to Professional Organizations
> Church Supplies (birthday cards, postage, etc.)
> Pastor's gifts "expected" to be given to members (wedding, baby, etc.)

> The "cost of a minister" is made up of appropriate employee benefits, provision for housing, and the actual cash salary paid . . . The list includes the type of basic employee benefits that should be provided in a well-balanced compensation plan:

> Social Security
> Tax-sheltered Annuity
> Health Insurance
> Dental Insurance
> Group Term Life Insurance
> Long-term Disability Insurance
> Accidental Death & Dismemberment Insurance
> Cash Bonuses
> Paid Holidays
> Vacation

> The "cost of a minister" also includes the provision for housing: a cash housing allowance, a parsonage plus utilities, or a combination of the two.[2]

Some organizations have stated goals and objectives for compensating their pastors. The Church of the Nazarene states its compensation policy in its *Manual:*

> Our compensation policy will attract, retain, reward, and motivate a pastor in a fair and equitable manner, when considering the

Annual Compensation of Senior Pastor by Worship Attendance

Church Attendance	0-99	100-299	300-499	500-749	750-999	1,000+
Number of Respondents	205	700	327	173	84	143
Salary (98%*)	20,049	27,566	34,787	38,941	44,964	45,551
Annual % Increase (66%)	8%	6%	5%	5%	5%	5%
Parsonage (25%)	7,175	8,393	9,837	9,939	16,220	13,747
Housing (80%)	9,380	12,714	16,507	19,238	21,064	24,449
Retirement (69%)	3,224	4,014	4,442	4,746	5,414	6,074
Life Insurance (33%)	1,247	1,321	1,986	843	968	1,376
Health Insurance (76%)	3,976	4,580	5,033	5,278	5,393	5,585
Vacation/weeks (94%)	3	3	4	4	4	4
Education Funds (47%)	850	921	1,186	1,341	1,266	1,616
Receive Auto Allow. (73%)	65%	68%	76%	83%	86%	82%

*The percentage following each compensation item indicates the portion of all senior pastors who received that form of compensation. The averages in each column are for those individuals who actually received that compensation item. Auto allowance is included as part of base salary.

Taken from *The 1997 Compensation Handbook for Church Staff.*

compensation of all pastors in the Church of the Nazarene, all pastors on the district, and the community and the members of the local congregation.

In light of those goals and objectives, the local church board may consider some specific objectives when extending a call to the pastoral team, such as:

1. Attracting a pastor who has a record of leading growing churches.
2. Increasing the pastor's average tenure in the local church.
3. Motivating the pastor to do what is necessary to cause the church to meet its objectives as an organization.

A local church board should consider the welfare of its pastoral team as a Christian obligation. It should also consider the fair and equitable financial support of the pastoral team to be wise stewards of God's resources.

What Are the Duties of the Pastoral Team

In some ways, the local church is not any different from any other organization that expects certain standards from those who are associated with it. In another sense, it is wholly different because a pastoral team's first duty and responsibility is to the Lord Jesus Christ. The pastor has been called by Christ and commissioned by His earthly Body, the Church.

However, the pastoral team does have an obligation to meet some organizational standards, directed and inspired by God, within the framework of the local church ministry. Some of those standards are exemplified in Jesus' parable of the Good Samaritan (Luke 10).

The Stewardship of Ministry

While Jesus was teaching the multitudes, there were a number of different people in His audience who disagreed with Him. Some came to trip Him up and to prove Him wrong.

A certain lawyer asked an insincere question, "'Teacher,' he asked, 'what must I do to inherit eternal life?'" (v. 25).

Since the lawyer was trained in the Law, Jesus referred him to the Law, "'What is written in the Law?' he replied. 'How do you read it?'" (v. 26).

The lawyer answered by quoting the Great Commandment (v. 27), "'Love the Lord your God with all your heart and with all your soul and with all your strength and with all your mind'; and, 'Love your neighbor as yourself.'"

Jesus referred to a standard. A person is required to give total allegiance to God with his or her emotional life, spiritual life, physical life, and mental life. The emphasis is "All your heart," which means total accountability to God. This is worked out in loving one's neighbor, not as one loves God but as you love yourself. The standard was not just self-love or pride. The standard was self-acceptance, self-worth. As a result, the neighbor should be accepted for what he or she is.

The nature of the discussion was stewardship. A person is accountable to manage his or her total obligation to God in four areas: (1) emotional, (2) spiritual, (3) physical, and (4) mental.

Just as the person was to love his or her neighbor as himself or herself, the "self" is the steward who is to manage his or her entire life for God.

The lawyer's answer was right. Jesus affirmed him, "You have answered correctly" (v. 28). However, Jesus didn't quite agree in His answer with the question that was asked. The lawyer had asked about "eternal life." Jesus answered, "Do this and you will live" (v. 28). To the lawyer, Jesus could have meant living in this world or living a good religious life. However, under the Old Testament dispensation, the one who loved God with all of his or her heart, soul, strength, and mind—and his or her neighbor as himself or herself—would have carried out the law to sacrifice and offer the blood atonement.

The discussion doesn't end. The lawyer "wanted to justify himself" (v. 29a), so he continued the conversation. Jesus had trapped him, so he wanted to get out of the trap. He wanted Jesus to answer the question, "Who is my neighbor?" (v. 29b). Probably the lawyer wanted Jesus to say that his neighbors were those who treated him like he treated them. Essentially, he wanted Jesus to say, "Those who keep the law as you keep the law are your neighbors."

If that was Jesus' answer, He would have reduced a person's stewardship to only those "religious" folks who obey the Law. In today's economy, that would have reduced a Christian's "ministry stewardship" to those in his or her Bible study—and probably not to all those in the local church. He or she would have only been responsible to, and accountable for, those who love God as he or she loved the Law.

But Jesus would not be caught in his trap. He realizes that every person has a stewardship of opportunity to every other person in the world. Because God created all, loves all (John 3:16), and sent us into all the world, we have a stewardship to all.

The pastoral team has a ministry to everyone they come in contact with, not just to those who treat them with love. They are to love the world as God loves the world, care for the world as God cares for the world, and minister to the world as God ministered to the world through the Lord Jesus Christ (Matt. 20:28).

John Wesley said, "Employ whatever God has entrusted you with, in doing good, all possible good, in every possible kind and degree, to the household of faith, to all men! This is no small part of 'the wisdom of the just.' Give all ye have, as well as all ye are, a spiritual sacrifice to Him who withheld not from you his Son, his only Son."[3]

In particular, there are several duties regarding "the household of faith" that the pastoral team should consider:

1. Divine authority. The pastoral team must seek heaven's authorization for its ministry, above and before any earthly authorization. A ministry born out of deep personal experience with God is an effective ministry.

A pastor received a large folded piece of paper in the mail. He unfolded the paper and saw there were two huge dots in the middle. Below the dots were the words, "Dear Pastor, this will help you in your ministry." The dots on the paper and the unsigned message puzzled the recipient. "This will help you in your ministry," the pastor reviewed the message, "I wonder what that means?" Throughout the rest of the busy day and into the evening hours, the pastor thought about those dots and the message, "This will help you in your ministry."

Later in the evening, while the pastor was reading, it suddenly hit him. He quickly went to his briefcase, took the paper out, unfolded it, and laid it on the floor. Tenderly, he knelt down on the paper. His knees almost fit perfectly with the dots. "This WILL help me in my ministry," he thought, as tears began to course down his face. A thoughtful child of God was used as a messenger to remind a busy pastor where his real authority came from.

The authority that comes from a "warmed heart" is one that will ignite the fires of faith in the lives of others. Moses asked about his authority to lead the Israelites in a time of soul searching and seeking the counsel of God. "Moses said to God, 'Suppose I go to the Israelites and say to them, "The God of your fathers has sent me to you," and they ask me, "What is his name?" Then what shall I tell them?' God said to Moses, 'I AM WHO I AM. This is what you are to say to the Israelites: "I AM has sent me to you"'" (Exod. 3:13-14).

Moses' credibility came from his reverence, obedience, and allegiance to God. The people weren't impressed by his past achievements in Pharaoh's kingdom; they were impressed by a face that shone from being in the presence of the divine. A ministerial commission born from a personal experience with the Lord Jesus Christ, and sealed by the anointing of the Holy Spirit, will make a greater impact than the clergy credentials of any earthly organization.

This is not to diminish the importance of the laying on of hands by the church. But it is an acknowledgment that the hand of God on the heart and life of the ministry bears greater influence than a mere human ceremony.

There will be times during the inevitable storms when ministers will doubt their calling. There will be times when some members of the congregation will "second the motion," but the call of God is greater than the calamity. The ordination service includes the mandate, "take authority to preach the Word." It is the minister's first duty to know God—to minister by the authority of his or her proximity to God. That knowledge is the source of all ministry strengths and the knowledge that will be verified most by the congregation.

"When they saw the courage of Peter and John and realized that they were unschooled, ordinary men, they were astonished and they took note that these men had been with Jesus" (Acts 4:13).

John Wesley was known to be a man of "one book." In his journal, he describes an incident where an associate sent him a discouraging letter. The content of the letter, Wesley said, "Threw me into great perplexity, till, after crying to God, I took up a Bible, which opened on these words: 'And Jabez called on the God of Israel, saying, O that thou wouldest bless me indeed, and enlarge my coast, and that thine hand might be with me, and that thou wouldest keep me from evil, that it may not grieve me! And God granted him that which he requested' (1 Chron. 4:10)."[4]

2. Preaching and teaching. A minister is called to preach and teach the Bible as God's inspired, infallible, and inerrant Word. The minister of God isn't called to scatter the seed of pop theology, church growth trends, or feel-good philosophies. A minister's duty is, first and foremost, to spread the seed of God's Word.

John Wesley wrote, "Let me then speak as a little child! Let my religion be plain, artless, simple! Meekness, temperance, patience, faith, and love, be these my highest gift; And let the highest words wherein I teach them, be those I learn from the book of God!"[5]

The local church has a right to see the prominent display of God's Word in the life and teaching of the pastoral team. One of the requirements for ministry outlined by the apostle Paul for young Timothy is that an "overseer must be . . . able to teach" (1 Tim. 3:2). The pastoral team must have a firsthand knowledge of God's Word and be able to communicate that knowledge through preaching and teaching. Wesley said, "Wherever a flock is duly fed with the pure milk of the word, they will be ready (were it possible) to pluck out their eyes, and give them to those that are over them in the Lord."[6]

3. The care of the church family. The care and feeding of the flock is an integral part of the ministry. Oftentimes, the feeding is easier than the caring. That's reflected in another of Wesley's journal entries, "I supposed my journeys this winter had been over, but I could not decline one more. Monday, 17, I set out for poor Colchester, to encourage the little flock."[7] Caring for the congregation involves leading people *to* Christ, teaching them *about* Christ, and leading them to be more *like* Christ. It also includes encouraging them to be diligent in worship, faithful in service, and loving in their fellowship with other Christians.

The pastoral team is responsible for leading the congregation in worship. Those worship times must be the object of prayerful planning to meet the various needs of the congregation.

Another key responsibility of the pastoral team is to encourage the congregation to strengthen their ties with the local church through assimilation and church membership.

The "Field of Dreams" philosophy must quickly be abandoned. The idea that "if we build it, they will come" is disastrous. Building a comfortable worship facility is not a substitute for building caring relationships with people. The pastoral team must go to the people. People do want to "know how much you care," but they also want you to "be there." Pastoral care is best done *in person*.

A thousand well-crafted sermons may be forgotten, but a hurting family will never forget the presence of a pastoral staff member sitting with them in a hospital room. A thousand well-planned lessons may be forgotten, but a confused and embarrassed family will never forget the presence of the minister sitting beside them in a courtroom when their friend or loved one faces the laws of the land. The Good Shepherd went to find the lost lamb. He didn't call

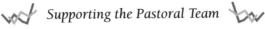

a committee meeting and plan a "Feed-the-lambs Sunday"; He went personally to seek the welfare of the missing lamb. Spirit-anointed programming is important to ministry, but programs must never be substituted for personal attention.

4. **Organizational responsibilities.** The pastor is called to supervise the ministry of laypersons. Leadership skills that include instruction, supervision, correction, and recognition are vital. At times, the administrative aspect of the ministry is most difficult. The pastoral team must have good people skills and a heart in tune with the leadership of the Holy Spirit.

"The pastor must know how to enlist laypersons, train them for their assignment, and supervise their efforts with love and encouragement."

—Towns/Toler

In a growing organization, the pastor equips the 20 percent 80 percent of the time. He or she is a leader—training the people who have been involved in everything. Such a pastor knows that leadership is influence, so he or she finds the people who are able to influence others. Then he or she serves the other 80 percent of the people 20 percent of the time. This pastor is a modeler. Instead of running milk routes, putting a bottle into a screaming mouth, burping babies and changing diapers, all of a sudden he or she begins to minister to people who can, in turn, minister to others. The church becomes a place of participants—partners in ministry, rather than an arena of spectators.[8]

5. **Intercessory prayer.** The pastoral team knows no higher privilege than to take its people before the throne of God in prayer. In his letter to Gaius, a friend and leader in the church, the apostle John assured him of his prayers, "Dear friend, I pray that you may enjoy good health and that all may go well with you, even as your soul is getting along well" (3 John 2). For the disciples, the mention of prayer was more than a formal greeting. They knew the young believers and leaders in their charge would need the protection and power of God over them. They faced unusual political op-

position, as well as the spiritual opposition of their chief enemy, the devil. They needed to know that someone was representing their cause to heaven.

The apostle Paul reminded the church at Thessalonica of his prayers, "We always thank God for all of you, mentioning you in our prayers. We continually remember before our God and Father your work produced by faith, your labor prompted by love, and your endurance inspired by hope in our Lord Jesus Christ" (1 Thess. 1:2-3).

John Wesley revealed his sentiments about intercessory prayer in his journal. While his brother Charles was speaking, Mr. Wesley gathered a prayer group to support him in intercessory prayer, "About two in the afternoon, being the time my brother was preaching at Oxford, before the University, I desired a few persons to meet with me, and join in prayer. We continued therein much longer than we at first designed, and believed we had the petition we asked of God."[9]

Those who serve under the supervision of the pastoral team have a right to know that their ministry is the subject of prayer.

Great Opportunity! Great Ministry!

The pastoral team has an awesome responsibility to reach its community for Jesus Christ, and then to enlist and train others to take the gospel to the rest of the world. Psychologist Dennis Waitley reminds us of each day's opportunity: "Each human being has exactly the same number of hours and minutes every day. Rich people can't buy more hours. Scientists can't invent new minutes. And you can't save time and spend it on another day. Even so, time is amazingly fair and forgiving. No matter how much time you've wasted in the past, you still have an entire tomorrow. Success depends upon using it wisely by planning and setting priorities."[10]

Jesus modeled pastoral ministry during His brief time on the earth. His teaching is both an encouragement and a challenge to every pastoral team member. The Samaritan woman at the well met the Master, and her life was changed in a moment. She went home to tell her countrymen, and they sought the One who had made the difference. As a result, Jesus was so besieged by seekers, He didn't even have time to eat. The disciples were naturally concerned and sought to bring Him some food. His answer revealed a heart filled with love for the needy, and gave every Christian worker a lesson in ministry priorities: "'My food,' said Jesus, 'is to do the will of him who sent me and to finish his work. Do you not say, "Four months more and then the harvest"? I tell you, open your eyes and look at the fields! They are ripe for harvest. Even now the reaper draws his wages, even now he harvests the crop for eternal life, so that the sower and the reaper may be glad together. Thus the saying "One sows and another reaps" is true. I sent you to reap what you have not worked for. Others have done the hard work, and you have reaped the benefits of their labors'" (John 4:34-38).

Notice several important ministry priorities in the scripture passage:

Priority One: Fulfilling the Great Commission! "My food . . . is to do the will of him who sent me and to finish his work" (v. 34). We live in an age of causes—from "save the seals" to "ban the bomb." And those causes have invaded the hearts and calendars of the members and attenders in every church.

Some of those causes are worthy, and many are utterly worthless in comparison to what really matters. Jesus reminded the disciples of the most important cause—more important than the basics of life itself. The cause: souls. The pastoral team must never forget its first obligation is evangelism.

In what is known as the Great Commission, Jesus forever established ministry priorities. "All authority in heaven and on earth has been given to me. Therefore go and make disciples of all nations, baptizing them in the name of the Father and of the Son and of the Holy Spirit, and teaching them to obey everything I have commanded you. And surely I am with you always, to the very end of the age" (Matt. 28:18-20).

Jesus told His disciples that He was finishing the work the Father gave Him to do. Obviously, the earthly part of that work is now in the hands of the believer. The One who announced that He was the "light of the world" gave the commission to His followers, "You are the light of the world. A city on a hill cannot be hidden" (Matt. 5:14).

The purpose for every sermon: *souls*.

The purpose for every song: *souls*.

The purpose for every Sunday School lesson: *souls*.

Priority Two: Harvest now! "Lift up your eyes and look at the fields, for they are already white for harvest!" (John 4:35, NKJV). As usual, Jesus' followers looked at the temporal instead of the eternal. Those around Jesus heard Him talk about a harvest, and they immediately thought about the harvest of crops that was well on schedule and only "four" months away.

Jesus saw a different harvest. He looked at the fields full of

Samaritan seekers making their way toward Him. He knew they were hungry for the peace and forgiveness the woman at the well had experienced. He knew He was the only answer for the forgiveness of their past and the hope for their future.

It was a pressing harvest. There were only a few days left before the earthly finality of Calvary. The work needed to be finished while there was still time.

It's a lesson for every minister who fills in a calendar. The big question: "What event on this calendar doesn't relate to the harvest?" If one is found, careful consideration should be made to its immediate removal!

Salvation is in the now, "I tell you, now is the time of God's favor, now is the day of salvation" (2 Cor. 6:2).

Priority Three: Celebrate your victories! "Both he who sows and he who reaps may rejoice together" (John 4:36, NKJV). The New Testament teaches us that there are various gifts for ministry that are divided among the ministers. Some ministers seem to be more gifted than others, however. And some seem to gain more recognition for the very same gift that is found in another.

The good news is found in Jesus' words, "rejoice together" (NKJV). For the faithful, the ground will be level on payday! The writer to the Hebrews promised, "God is not unjust; he will not forget your work and the love you have shown him" (6:10).

There are different gifts and different honors, but both will receive the same reward.

Priority Four: Pass the faith along! "Others have labored, and you have entered into their labors" (John 4:38, NKJV). Phineas F. Bresee said, "We are debtors to give the gospel to every person in the same manner in which we have received it." Sharing Christ is the one thing everyone can learn to do. There may be different styles and methods, but the work can still be done by the youngest and the oldest in the faith.

The apostle said to Timothy, "The things you have heard me say in the presence of many witnesses entrust to reliable men who will also be qualified to teach others" (2 Tim. 2:2). Members of the pastoral team should see themselves as a God-anointed link in the chain of the gospel.

It will make a difference then, to understand that everything that is learned is learned so that it may be taught to someone else.

In the cause of the Great Commission, every ministry is transferable.

EXPANDING THE GIVING BASE

Command them to do good, to be rich in good deeds, and to be generous and willing to share. In this way they will lay up treasure for themselves as a firm foundation for the coming age, so that they may take hold of the life that is truly life (1 Tim. 6:18-19).

> **"The only safe rule is to give more than we can spare."**
> —C. S. Lewis

A NEW YORK CITY HIGH SCHOOL TEACHER decided to honor her graduating seniors by telling them what a difference each of them had made in her life. Using an honor system developed by Helice Bridges of Del Mar, California, she called her students to the front of the class and told each of them how they had made the difference to her and to the class. Then she presented each of them a blue ribbon with an imprinted message, "Who I Am Makes a Difference."

The ribbon ceremony made such an impression the teacher decided to expand the recognition by including other members of the community. She gave each student in her class a blue ribbon and asked them to find a special person to honor.

One of the students went to her supervisor in a nearby factory where she worked part time. Her supervisor had been especially helpful to her and always seemed to have an encouraging word.

The student explained, "My high school teacher asked me to give a blue ribbon to someone who has made a difference in my life." As the student pinned the ribbon on her supervisor's shirt, she said, "Mrs. Atkins, you really have made a difference in my life. I appreciate all you've done for me."

The supervisor blushed as the ribbon was pinned on, and the student continued, "Mrs. Atkins, here's another ribbon. Would you do me a favor and find someone else who deserves a blue ribbon and give it to them?" Thanking the worker, she replied, "That's a great idea!"

"Oh, and one other thing," the worker said, "will you take an extra ribbon with you and tell them to give the extra ribbon to someone else?"

The supervisor agreed to the request and went to the office of her boss, the factory's vice president. She didn't know exactly how he would react to the blue ribbon ceremony since he had a reputation for being the "factory grouch."

"Sir," she began as she pointed to her ribbon, "one of our part-time workers just gave me this blue ribbon and told me that I had made a difference in her life."

"And," she continued, "she asked me to give this ribbon to someone who has made a difference in my life." The boss looked surprised as the supervisor walked over and pinned a blue ribbon on his jacket, "Mr. Samson, I want you to have this ribbon because you've made a difference in my life. I know this has been a difficult month for the company, but I've always admired your patience and your hard work. You've been very helpful to me and to my department. I appreciate you." The boss fumbled for words, "Uh . . . well . . . uh . . . thank you. I'll wear it with honor."

"By the way," the supervisor continued as she handed a second ribbon to her boss, "here's another ribbon. Why not give it to someone who's made a difference in your life."

"I will," the boss responded, as he thanked her again for the honor.

Later in the evening, the boss went to his teenage son's room. The door was locked, and he assumed the boy was working on a homework assignment. He knocked, "Son, could I come in for a moment?" The door opened, "Sure, Dad. What's the problem?" "No problem," the father continued, "I had the most awesome thing happen to me at work today."

"What's that?" the boy replied. The father answered, "Someone pinned a blue ribbon on me and asked me to give this ribbon to someone that had made a difference in my life."

"Come here, Son," the father invited, "I have a ribbon for you." As he pinned the ribbon on his son he said, "I know we haven't had much time to spend together, with all the problems at work and stuff. And I know I don't tell you this enough, but I really do appreciate you. When that worker asked me to give a ribbon to someone who made a difference in my life, you came to mind right away. Your mother and I love you so very much."

Tears began to chase each other down the boy's face as he replied, "Thanks, Dad."

"Dad, before you go, there's something I have to tell you."

"What's that, Son?" the father wondered.

"Things haven't been going so great for me either. I had a fight with my best friend at school, and today, my girlfriend told me she was breaking up with me. And I guess I'll have to say, I even wondered if you cared about me. Dad, this afternoon I decided to end it all. I was writing you and mom a note." He looked down at the ribbon on his shirt and read it out loud, "Who I Am Makes a Difference." "Thanks, Dad," the son reached for his father, "I really needed that!"

Christian giving is like the story. One sincere gift prompts another. Our giving sends out ripples of influence like the tiny waves emanating from the source where the pebble is thrown into a pond. John Bunyan said through one of his famous characters, "The more he cast away, the more he had."

An old epitaph reads, "What I gave, I have; what I spent, I had; what I kept, I lost." That's the attitude that will "make a difference."

The opposite of that spirit of giving is seen in the story of a man who was taking a daily walk as part of a regimen recommended by his physician after a heart attack. At home, the telephone rang and his wife answered. On the other end of the line was the representative from the Reader's Digest Sweepstakes. The call was to inform the gentleman, known for his "frugality," that he had just won the sweepstakes and a certified check for $1 million would be arriving.

The wife was ecstatic. All of their dreams would come true. All of their bills would soon be paid, and they would have opportunity for investments beyond their wildest dreams!

Then she suddenly thought of how the news would affect her husband. "Will the news give him another heart attack?" she thought. After a good deal of thought, she decided to call their pastor for some advice. Surely the pastor would know how to handle these difficult decisions.

"Pastor, I just received the news that my husband has won the Reader's Digest Sweepstakes," she said. "What on earth do I do now!"

The pastor was a bit confused by the question he had just heard over the telephone. He knew what he might be doing if he had won. "That's great!" the pastor replied to the wife. "But what seems to be the problem?"

In a worried tone, the wife answered, "I'm afraid my husband will have another heart attack when I give him the news. He may even die!"

The pastor said, "I'll be right there."

The husband returned from his walk to see the pastor's car in front of the house. He rushed inside and was met by the pastor. "What's wrong, Pastor?"

"Now calm down, Ed," the pastor assured the worried husband. "Ed, I've got a little problem I need to discuss with you."

The husband responded, "Pastor, you know I'll help you any way I can. What is it?"

Taking a deep breath, the pastor continued, "Ed, it's a problem about stewardship. Let me give you an example. What if a person like you suddenly received word that he had won a million dollars. What would you do with all that money?"

The husband smiled and put his hand on the pastor's shoulder. "That's easy, Pastor. You know the first thing I would do is give $750,000 of it to the church."

Hearing his answer, the pastor had a massive heart attack and dropped dead!

All church leaders may not react in the same way, but many of them would be delighted to hear about that kind of loyalty among their parishioners. With rising costs and lowering commitments, church leaders are concerned about funding the church's ministry—both short-term and long-term.

The Sunday morning offering plate can no longer be viewed as the only time and place to seek financial support for the church. Stewardship goes beyond Sunday. Stewardship is a lifestyle, not an event. The writer of Ecclesiastes reminds, "When God gives any man wealth and possessions, and enables him to enjoy them, to accept his lot and be happy in his work—this is gift of God" (5:19). That contentment can be seen in these words:

> Take my love, my God, I pour
> At Thy feet its treasure store.
> Take myself and I will be
> Ever, only, all for Thee;
> Ever, only, all for Thee.
> —Frances R. Havergal

"Giving Dying"

State and federal laws make it possible to give not only while we live but also after we're gone. The principle of "Giving living" may be extended to include "Giving dying," through careful planning and the wise use of God's resources. It truly is possible for someone to "give—and give—and give," even beyond this lifetime.

Church leaders concerned about developing a giving church should give careful consideration to educating their congregations about planned giving. It is a biblical way to expand the giving base of the local church and continue the spiritual influence of the giver at the same time.

Daniel D. Busby, Kent E. Barber, and Robert L. Temple, authors of *The Christian's Guide to Worry-Free Money Management*, advise, "It is not only important how you spend your money during your lifetime, it is also important to make provisions for its wise use after your death."[1]

Dr. Steve Weber, director of Stewardship Development Ministries for the Church of the Nazarene, often tells the story of a young man who was asked to build a house for his boss, sparing no expense in materials and workmanship. Ignoring his boss's instructions, he cut corners everywhere. Upon his return, the boss called the young builder in and surprised him with the announcement that the house was a gift to him. The house now belonged to the builder. The authors remind that unwise financial building also affects those who survive us.

A church or organization's giving base may be greatly enhanced by the contributions of those members who have been instructed in the importance of giving beyond their lifetime.

The Church of the Nazarene has received nearly $40 million in special gifts and bequests through wills and trusts. Two of those gifts exceeded $1 million, but the average gift was over $16,000.

There are people in your congregation who could give more to the church after their death than they ever will while they are alive.

Those stewards who gave to their denomination, gave from their assets and not from their income. Estate gifts (gifts or assets) are typically larger than gifts from income. Good stewardship involves giving God a portion in return for His blessings during their lifetime, and even at their death.

Ray Lyne, author and financial consultant, said in a stewardship training seminar in Columbus, Ohio, "God has not stated in the Scriptures that faithful stewardship is only for those who have accumulated large amounts of wealth. In fact," he adds, "one of the greatest compliments He gave to a steward was to the widow who had little to give, but was faithful with what she had."

Who Benefits from Special Gifts and Bequests?

Roger Alexander, director of Planned Giving in the Church of the Nazarene, reported in a study of more than 5,000 wills, it was revealed that 66 percent of the dollars given went to the local church, 2 percent to district organizations, 12 percent to colleges, universities, or Bible colleges, and 20 percent to general church ministries.

The statistics reveal several things: (1) people love their local churches; (2) alumni remember their alma maters; (3) members appreciate the work of their denominational ministries; (4) people don't make stewardship decisions in one day but over a long time, because relationships have been developed.

According to the American Association of Fund-Raising Counsel (AAFRC), of the $144 billion that was given to charity during a recent year, the gifts were distributed as follows:

Charity	Percent
Religion	44
Education	13
Health	9
Arts	7
Other[2]	14
Unallocated	5

In response to one denomination's survey question, "Have you considered remembering the church in your stewardship plan?" 50 percent indicated that they had included their local church in their will. They saw the advantage of giving beyond their lifetime in a prayerful, planned, and purposeful way.[3]

Should Your Church Use a Stewardship Planning Service?

Inviting an approved representative to conduct a stewardship planning service in your church can help you expand your giving base and benefit the church member's family at the same time. If a planned giving specialist is invited to speak at your church, Steve Weber recommends that the presentation should cover the following topics:

1. The importance of Christian stewardship
2. The value of financial planning
3. Recommended resources for estate planning
4. Information and brochures on a variety of stewardship matters
5. The importance of a will
6. The recommendation of qualified consultants and agencies

Facilitating the Planning Process

Larry Carr, president of the Presbyterian Church (U.S.A.), is quoted in a *Christianity Today* article by Keith Hinson, "The most basic strategy should be for denominations to maintain strong programs that encourage older Christians to bequeath assets to churches. Not having a program like this is probably the best example of poor stewardship I could offer. It is not being faithful harvesters of the glorious field in which God has placed us."[4]

Larry Burkett says in his book *Your Finances in Changing Times:*

> Many Christians have the ability to accumulate large amounts of wealth. Virtually everyone in America has the potential of accumulating a surplus. What we consider to be a minimum standard of living is significantly above that experienced in most other parts of the world. It is not unheard of for someone living on a small fixed income to accumulate tens of thousands of dollars through scrimping and sacrificing. With that potential, it becomes vital that God's attitude about accumulating money becomes a part of our personalities.[5]

But there is much competition for that wealth—even focused on the parishioners of your church. Your church is a marketing target! Commercial and charitable organizations understand that your parishioners respond to their pleas. The Direct Marketing Association suggested to their members, "Look for new donors in churches and other houses of worship, no matter whether your organization is religious or not."[6]

It is important to make the congregation aware of the long-term needs of the local church and to give them the opportunity to meet those needs in their stewardship planning. Church members must also be educated as to the importance of long-term giving to the local church for four important reasons:

1. The church is the center of spiritual development for the entire family.
2. The church is a lighthouse to the unchurched in each city.
3. The church impacts the morals and values of their communities.
4. The church provides a spiritual heritage for each generation.

The Value of Helping People Plan for Tomorrow

Church leaders should be taught about the four "Fs" of stewardship planning.

The first is **family.** Who will be impacted after the death of a church member? A spouse? Children? The church? Are survivors aware of the stewardship plans? The apostle Paul gave Timothy a rather stern warning about providing for his family, "If anyone does not provide for his relatives, and especially for his immediate family, he has denied the faith and is worse than an unbeliever" (1 Tim. 5:8).

The second is **finances.** What assets has God entrusted the congregants to accomplish the plans He has given? Are their plans too big for their possessions? Are their possessions too big for their plans?

God gives graciously to His children. James wrote, "Every good and perfect gift is from above, coming down from the Father of the heavenly lights, who does not change like shifting shadows" (1:17).

God has brought many "treasures" into our lives. He has not only enriched us with spiritual blessings but given us material blessing as well. And we are called to be wise stewards of those blessings/possessions, not only by the wise use of them during our lifetime, but also in the wise assignment of them after our death.

Parishioners must be taught not to take their possessions lightly. That house that seems far too small for their needs at times would be considered a mansion to a family in South America living between four walls of scrap metal, near a garbage dump. That used, compact car that seems most at home in the mechanic's garage would be considered a limousine to someone in a Far Eastern country whose only transportation has been a used bicycle.

There is a popular public television program that broadcasts from various antique show locales. Show exhibitors and attenders present items from their collections to expert appraisers who have been secured by the show's producers. In a matter of moments, what seemed to be an insignificant artifact may be determined by the appraisers to be an antique "treasure" worth, in many instances, several thousand dollars.

As each "treasure" is revealed, the collector usually shows a great deal of surprise. He or she assumed that there was value in that particular possession but didn't know how far that value exceeded his or her assumption!

Every possession was graciously and generously given to us by a Heavenly Father who promised to supply our needs. They have been given to us for management purposes. Neil Strait said, "A kind of stewardship so necessary in the contemporary world is the proper handling of our resources. Too often they are handled carelessly and without concern for others, or for the future. A good steward knows that all the things of life are important. He or she handles them with care and with respect, knowing that someday they will pass to others."[7]

A steward can presume on God's resources, or even waste them. For instance, the steward in Jesus' parable of the talents wasted his talent by doing nothing. And, by doing nothing, the talent didn't earn interest or multiply. The folly of such presumption would be comparable to taking a stack of one hundred dollar bills and hiding them in a mattress. That same stack of bills invested in a mutual fund, for example, may gain interest, or if it were invested, it could double, triple, or even increase a hundredfold.

A man was once asked to invest $50,000 to get Wendy's started. He knew Dave Thomas and knew him to be an outstanding manager. But he doubted if anyone could go head-to-head with McDonald's, so he refused to put money into the Wendy's hamburger chain. Today, had the man invested $50,000 in Wendy's, it would be worth over $5 million.

The third is **facts.** Everyone has three places to distribute their resources: (1) family and friends, (2) charity, or (3) the government. Your parishioners may be asked some important questions about their inheritance. Can their children handle receiving all of their inheritance at once? Would it be better if family members received their inheritance later?

Another question relates to taxes. Do they want to avoid paying any tax? Or, do they want to pay some of the inheritance taxes? Everyone has similar choices to make when it comes to stewardship planning. The extent to which parishioners give thoughts and actions to their choices determines the effect of our stewardship.

Do they want to rely upon joint ownership?

What about lawsuits, divorced children, or gift tax issues?

Peter Drucker said, "Long-range planning does not deal with the future decisions but with the future of present decisions." Procrastination is everyone's biggest enemy in stewardship planning.

Also remember that the best-laid plans mean nothing unless they have been put into an up-to-date, written, legal format, and executed in a proper manner.

A fourth is **facilitator**. Every stewardship plan needs the oversight of trusted professional advisers to ensure that intended plans are carried out in a legal and equitable way. "Plans fail for lack of counsel, but with many advisers they succeed" (Prov. 15:22).

Resourcing the Giver Who Plans

We live in a wonderful age! Resources are readily available to anyone who wants to plan wisely for the future.

Roger Alexander often lectures about **popular deferred gifts**. Roger's list invariably includes the following:

1. **Last wills and testaments.** Seventy percent of the estate gifts given to the church come through last wills and testaments.
2. **New and existing life insurance policies.** A very popular source of investment, over $9 trillion in life insurance is currently in force. Making the church a beneficiary of a life insurance policy benefits both the donor and the church.
3. **Revocable living trusts (a.k.a. grantor trusts).** Your parishioners may also give to the church by establishing a "trust" in which he or she transfers, or gives, property "in trust" for his or her own benefit, or the benefit of others. The trust is "revocable" (changeable) until either the donor expires or the end of a predetermined period of time.
4. **Charitable remainder trusts.** The charitable remainder

trust is an arrangement that grants "remainder interest" to a legal charity. *Fixed* or *variable* income procedures can be established to the advantage of the donor or the beneficiary. Your parishioner can "lock in" a gift to the church now, and continue to benefit from the trust in several ways.

5. **Charitable gift annuities.** Members can transfer money or property to the church in return for the organization's agreement to pay the donor a fixed payment for life.

6. **Life estate agreements.** A life estate agreement is a legal arrangement whereby the beneficiary (i.e., the life tenant) gives real property to the church but yet is entitled to the income from the property for his or her lifetime. Upon the death of the "life tenant," the property will be transferred to the holder of the "remainder interest." The steward-benefactor can give away his or her home and still live in it! There is also the knowledge that the beneficiary organization will receive the real property when it is no longer needed.

7. **Qualified retirement plans.** Over $5 trillion in qualified retirement plans now exist, allowing individuals, whether or not they are covered by qualified pension or profit-sharing plans, to set aside a certain amount of their income each year. IRAs and their equivalents are currently the number one savings vehicle.

8. **Totten trusts (a.k.a. pay on death [P.O.D.] and transfer on death [T.O.D.] designations).** Church leaders can create a Totten trust by depositing money (in some states, bank accounts, as well as vehicles and land, can be transferred or designated as P.O.D. or T.O.D.) in their name as a trustee for another. Title is assigned to that trustee who holds it in a revocable trust for the beneficiary during the trustee's lifetime. At the "trustee's" death, the asset becomes the property of the person designated as the beneficiary.

"Don't give until it hurts, give until it feels good. Model in your family the face of a happy person investing in eternal values."

—Jim Priest

The **popular inter vivos gifts** (gifts made while the donor is living) is also a widely used method of estate planning.

The following methods are the most popular methods:

1. **Cash** is still the most popular way to give during a church member's lifetime. And it should also be noted that income tax deductions of up to 50 percent of the donor's *adjusted gross income* are available to those who itemize. This "ceiling on deductibility" is applicable for most donors to local churches.

2. **Long-term appreciated securities** (those held for more than one year, with a current fair market value that exceeds their cost basis). A church's giving base can also be expanded, and the donor's capital gains tax can possibly be avoided, by retitling securities (e.g., stocks) in the church's name and letting the church sell it. Because income tax deductions are based on the full, fair market value of the stock, income tax deductions of up to 30 percent of the donor's adjusted gross income are available to those donors who itemize.

3. **Long-term appreciated real property** (property held for more than one year with a current "fair market value" that exceeds its cost basis). A church's giving base may also be expanded by a member's *retitling* real property in the church's name and allowing the church to sell it. The donor will possibly avoid capital gains tax, and to those who itemize, income tax deductions of up to 30 percent of adjusted gross income are available.

4. **New and existing life insurance policies.** Major gifts can be made to the church for pennies on the dollar, if premiums continue to be paid over the required time period, by the transfer of life insurance policies.

5. **Tangible personal property.** It is possible for a person to give tangible personal property to the local church. It is property that may be "touched" or "felt" (e.g., a chair or a watch), in comparison to such property as automobiles, boats, planes, coins, guns, or jewelry.

Planned giving expert Roger Alexander estimates that up to $10 trillion will be transferred to the next generation by the year 2025, making it the largest intergenerational transfer of wealth the world has ever known.

Many of your parishioners will be included in that transfer.

And a wise stewardship plan will give them the opportunity to make some of the transfer funds available to your church. They must also be reminded that stewardship involves 100 percent of what we have, not simply the 10 percent tithe.

Current Thoughts and Trends (August 1998) quotes a *Washington Post Weekly* (May 11, 1998) article by Rajiv Chandrasekaran, "According to recent Federal Reserve estimates, United States businesses will spend an estimated $50 billion to correct year-2000 glitches in millions of computers." He adds, "The repair bill is projected to reach $300 billion" and "all corporate and government computers worldwide must be corrected because of the interdependence of machines in data exchange." And to summarize the scope of the preparation, he says, "A failure in one machine could cripple systems in other offices, states, or countries."

Likewise, a stewardship emphasis that focuses on just the *lifetime* giving of time, talent, and treasure could have a wide-range effect. Energies spent on educating parishioners to *give beyond their lifetime* might be the very thing that would keep your ministry from "shutting down" at a certain point in time.

The authors do not present the materials in this chapter as qualified legal advice. The design of the chapter is to be informative and helpful. The matter of planned giving is both complex and challenging. But, with wise counsel from the legal experts and from the Word of God, you will succeed.

Maybe you have heard the story of the Christian lady who had to do a lot of traveling for her business. Flying, in particular, made her nervous, so she always took her Bible along with her to read, and it helped relax her. On one occasion she was reading her Bible seated next to a man. When he saw her Bible, he laughed and went back to what he was doing.

After awhile, he turned to her and asked, "You don't really believe all that stuff in there, do you?"

The women responded, "Of course I do. It is the Bible."

He said, "Well, what about that guy that was swallowed by the whale?"

She replied, "Oh, Jonah. Yes, I believe that; it is in the Bible."

He asked, "Well, how do you suppose he survived all that time inside the whale?"

The lady said, "Well, I don't really know. I guess when I get to heaven, I will ask him."

"What if he isn't in heaven?" the man asked sarcastically.

"Then you ask him," replied the lady.

Hopefully, this delightful story illustrates the importance of believing the best and doing our best for God. The point is, we don't have to understand everything about planned giving to promote it!

I heard Joe Seaborn say in a message at Taylor County Camp, Butler, Georgia, "In a real sense, giving to the cause of Christ is nothing more or less than laying aside eternal investments so that when we stand before Christ in heaven, we have gold, silver, and precious stones that we have been laying at His feet all along. The crown that we talk about laying at His feet will just be one more thing that we give, our final offering, in a long string of offerings that began long before."

A Prayer of Those Who Care

I do not know how long I'll live;
But while I live, Lord, let me give
Some comfort to someone in need
By smile or nod—kind word or deed,
And let me do whate'er I can
To ease things for my fellowman.
I want naught but to do my part,
To lift a tired or weary heart—
To change folks' frowns to smiles again
Then I will not have lived in vain,
And I'll not care how long I'll live
If I can give—and give—and give!
—Anonymous

Yours, O Lord, is the greatness and the power and the glory and the majesty and the splendor, for everything in heaven and earth is yours. Yours, O Lord, is the kingdom; you are exalted as head over all. Wealth and honor come from you; you are the ruler of all things (1 Chron. 29:11-12).

APPENDIXES

*STEWARDSHIP
SERMONS*

Developing a Giving Environment
Luke 6:27-38

But I tell you who hear me: Love your enemies, do good to those who hate you, bless those who curse you, pray for those who mistreat you. If someone strikes you on one cheek, turn to him the other also. If someone takes your cloak, do not stop him from taking your tunic. Give to everyone who asks you, and if anyone takes what belongs to you, do not demand it back. Do to others as you would have them do to you.

If you love those who love you, what credit is that to you? Even "sinners" love those who love them. And if you do good to those who are good to you, what credit is that to you? Even "sinners" do that. And if you lend to those from whom you expect repayment, what credit is that to you? Even "sinners" lend to "sinners," expecting to be repaid in full. But love your enemies, do good to them, and lend to them without expecting to get anything back. Then your reward will be great, and you will be sons of the Most High, because he is kind to the ungrateful and wicked. Be merciful, just as your Father is merciful.

Do not judge, and you will not be judged. Do not condemn, and you will not be condemned. Forgive, and you will be forgiven. Give, and it will be given to you. A good measure, pressed down, shaken together and running over, will be poured into your lap. For with the measure you use, it will be measured to you.

Introduction

Love is the foundation for stewardship. As someone has well noted, "You can give without loving, but you cannot love without giving." Love is the motivation for everything we do, and this is particularly so in our stewardship.

One of the best-known verses in scripture teaches us that God loved us and gave to us. "For God so loved the world that he gave his one and only Son, that whoever believes in him shall not perish but have eternal life" (John 3:16). You cannot separate loving and giving because true love always leads to giving. The object of your love knows no limitations or constraints.

People think that if a person is a millionaire, he or she will give much to God. Experiences suggest that is probably not true. Giving has nothing to do with our financial state; it has everything to do with our love relationship to God. Those who love God the most make the greatest sacrifice for Him. This does not necessarily mean they give the largest monetary gift to God, although that is often the case. Giving is not measured by the amount of money given but by the sacrifice made for the purpose of giving. The widow who gave only two mites made the greatest sacrifice, because it was all she had.

The Integrity of a Giver

Because love is a characteristic of God in His very nature, it is expected that the same kind of love should be a part of the Christian's regenerated character. The apostle John twice reminded his readers that love was the characteristic of God and on both occasions he made specific application to the love life of the believer. First, he argued a person who does not love really does not have a personal relationship with God. "Whoever does not love does not know God, because God is love" (1 John 4:8). If we affirm God as a God of love, we must acknowledge that characteristic attribute must also be evident in our lives as believers.

There is, therefore, a world of difference between the giving of the Christian and the giving of the world. Christian giving is an expression and evidence of the indwelling love of God.

1. Giving environments generate good for evil. We Christians should return good for the evil we receive. The world says, "An eye for an eye," but as Christians, we take the shirts off our backs to give to others. We love our enemies and pray for those who mistreat us.

Little babies born into the world are nothing but consumers. They demand their rights, cry for attention, and want their needs met immediately. Yet we fall in love with those little babies and give everything we can to them. It is because these babies belong to us; it is natural to love them.

However, it is unnatural to love our enemies. How can we love them? There are two kinds of love—love of the heart and love of the will. When the Bible speaks of the love of the heart, it uses the Greek word *philanthropia,* which literally means "a brotherly love for humankind." Most often this word is translated "kindness" in Scripture. While that is part of Christian love, Christian love goes beyond heartfelt kindness and also includes the self-sacrificing *agape* love of the will. It is not natural to love an enemy out of our hearts. Even as Christians we find it difficult to turn our hearts toward enemies who want to hurt us. Christian love for enemies must come from the will.

God is the model for loving our enemies. "While we were still sinners, Christ died for us" (Rom. 5:8). When we love our enemies like the Father, we initiate good for evil.

Former American President Abraham Lincoln in many ways personified this aspect of Christian giving. He was often criticized for his positive treatment of his sworn enemies. One of Lincoln's enemies once stated in print he thought Lincoln was a mistake and the American public would live to regret placing such an obvious incompetent in the White House. The nature of the critic's attack on Lincoln even degenerated to the place where Lincoln's physical features were compared to those of a gorilla and the ape came out on top. Later, when war broke out between the States, Lincoln asked that critic to serve as his secretary of war.

Lincoln's advisers were appalled with the president's actions. When they asked him why he would choose his critic for such an important post, he responded he thought Staunton was the best man for the job. When they advised him that he should seek to destroy his enemies rather than treat them like friends, he reminded them he was destroying his enemies when he made them his friends. Later, when Lincoln died, Staunton was standing by the president's bedside. As he watched Lincoln breathe his last breath, he uttered the words, "There dies the greatest ruler of mankind the world has ever seen."

We will show our spiritual maturity by how we respond to those who have treated us wrongfully. It does not take spiritual maturity to treat others well who treat us well. Even the unsaved do that. Our ability to take adversity in a Christian spirit and return good for evil does take spiritual maturity.

2. Giving environments change society's values. When we give, society becomes a better place. When we are giving to missions, preaching the gospel, or teaching the Word of God, the influence of Christianity makes the world a better place.

We should treat others as we want them to treat us. The Golden Rule is found in some form in every religion of the world. A Jewish rabbi, Hillel, said, "What is hateful to thee, do not to another." An Alexandrian philosopher said, "What you hate to suffer, do not do to anyone else." Socrates said, "What things make you angry when you suffer them at the hands of others, do not do to those other people." The Stoics declared, "What you do not wish to be done to yourself, do not do to anyone else." Confucius said, "What you do not want done to yourself, do not do to others." The worldly statement of the Golden Rule is negative, "Don't do to others what would be uncomfortable to us." But the Christian adds the positive, "Do to others what you want done to you," which is God's standard. God wants us to do positive things, not just refrain from the negative things. We can refrain from the negative, but that does not make us godly. It is a lot easier not to do what we don't want to do than it is to do what we want to do. The Golden Rule as taught by Jesus is a healer of wrong relationships.

What do we want other people to do to for us? What are some of the positive things we want them to do to us?

▷ We want people to give us the benefit of the doubt.

▷ We want people to give us another opportunity to do better.

▷ We want people to admit that they make mistakes.

3. Giving environments generate depth in relationships. Christian giving is more than Christmas swapping with God or others. We often buy someone a Christmas gift because we think that person is going to buy us a gift. But that is not the Christian motivation. The world responds, but the Christian gives. The world responds because it is going to get something in return, but Christians give because they want to give. They give to others because God has given to them.

If we love only those who love us, that is not uniquely Christian. The world does that. The same with giving money. If we give to those who will give to us, that is not Christian. When Jesus said "expecting nothing in return," He was speaking of radical giving. And when our giving is based on love, it is fanatical and radical because it takes the dedication of our whole life.

We may try to use the excuse, "I cannot give to the church because I am in great debt," but our bank balance has nothing to do with giving to God. We may say that we must have money for ourselves and our families, therefore we cannot give to God. When we use our families as an excuse for not giving, it is a cop-out. More often, the reason for our financial bondage is a failure to discipline our lives. We have not learned that stewardship is management, and we are not managing our lives well. Usually, the resulting problems first show up in our financial affairs. When we begin applying the sound principles of biblical stewardship to life, we will give to God out of love and learn to discipline our lives. Then we will not only give that proportion that belongs to God but also manage the rest of our lives according to biblical principles. Well-managed lives glorify God.

4. Giving environments generate Christlike characteristics. The world invests its money according to that which will give a good return. This is not necessarily based on selfishness or hoarding; it is based on being good stewards of assets and resources. God believes in us, therefore He invests in us. Yet God invested in a product that, at the time of the investment, must have seemed a high risk and a subsequent low yield. The world system is not based on mercy but on merit. In other words, if you can do something for me, I will do something for you. Business is run by the merit system. Merit is based on giving value in return for money. But everyone who knows Jesus Christ is a product of the "mercy system" . . . we were saved by grace and not by works.

5. Giving environments bring unexpected blessings. Jesus promises, "Give, and it shall be given unto you" (Luke 6:38, KJV). We will get a blessing back when we give to others. By our standard of measure it will be measured to us in return. One person asked his minister, "How much should I give to God?" "How much do you want in life?" the minister replied. When another person asks his pastor if he should base his proportionate giving on his net or gross income, the wise minister responded with a question, "Do you want a net or gross blessing from God?" God gives to us based on how we give to Him. We can't outgive God because He multiplies our gift in His work and returns it to us accordingly. We have little blessing from God when we invest very little with God. We must learn the stewardship of giving.

The Lifestyle of a Giver

There is more to Christian giving than certain characteristic acts that might seem to be otherwise unnatural. Because Christian giving is an expression of the indwelling love of God, there is often a spirit accompanying the act of love that is better experienced than told. The open hand that gives to the needs of others is accompanied by an open heart of compassion that is the original motive in giving.

1. A relational lifestyle. Christian giving is more than isolated acts of kindness to those in need. It is a constant spiritual lifestyle. Giving money to God is not a one-time event but rather a continual attitude that affects the process of life. Jesus did not talk about going with someone the second mile or giving someone our coats as a one-time act. He was talking about an attitude that becomes a part of our way of life. Some of us will keep count of our giving with an attitude of quitting when we hit a certain point. Then we quit giving and expect others to take over for us. But Christian giving does not keep score, nor does it keep a balance sheet. We give to God because we love Him. As we grow in our love we will grow in our giving, and as we grow in giving we will also grow in our love for God because where your treasure is, there your heart will be also.

2. A lifestyle encompassed by grace. It takes grace to be that kind of consistent giver, and that grace can only come from God. Jesus described the giver who gives by grace and not by grit. If His disciples had been merely poor, they may have been able to make some sacrifices, roll up their shirtsleeves, grit their teeth, and give to God. But these disciples were poor and therefore could not obey Jesus' command to give even if they wanted to, apart from the grace of God.

Have you ever noticed how many of the biblical examples of giving were individuals who gave out of their deep poverty? As we mature in other graces in the Christian life, God wants us to excel in the grace of giving.

Conclusion

Years ago a Sunday School missionary preached in a church and made his appeal for funds to help buy books that could be used in starting new Sunday Schools in the American frontier. As others gave money for the cause, one little girl wanted to help reach boys and girls through Sunday Schools but had no money to give. As the offering plate was passed down her aisle, she slipped her prize possession in life, her mother's gold wedding band, off her finger and placed it in the offering plate. After the service, a businessman came to the missionary deeply moved by the little girl's sacrifice. He had seen the girl silently place the ring in the offering plate and knew it represented the memory of her recently deceased mother. The man offered to redeem the ring for far more than it was worth, if the missionary agreed to return the ring to the orphan girl. But when the missionary tried to return it, she refused, noting she had given it to help purchase books to start Sunday Schools that would reach boys and girls and tell them about Jesus. When she could not be persuaded to take back the ring, the missionary kept it and used it as an object lesson as he presented the cause of the Sunday School mission. Over the years, the missionary retold the story many times. The little girl's example of sacrifice resulted in raising thousands of dollars needed for the expansion of this missionary endeavor.

God wants us to be a blessing and receive a blessing by giving to Him out of our poverty so He can enrich our lives. It is easy to find reasons why we cannot afford to give to God, but that only hinders Him in His desire to bless us. When we realize the great resources of the world God has at His disposal, it is obvious God does not want us to give because He needs or wants our money. God wants us to learn the stewardship of giving so that He can be justified in abundantly blessing our lives.

Developing Stewardship Plans
Matt. 6:19-34

Do not store up for yourselves treasures on earth, where moth and rust destroy, and where thieves break in and steal. But store up for your-selves treasures in heaven, where moth and rust do not destroy, and where thieves do not break in and steal. For where your treasure is, there your heart will be also.

The eye is the lamp of the body. If your eyes are good, your whole body will be full of light. But if your eyes are bad, your whole body will be full of darkness. If then the light within you is darkness, how great is that darkness!

No one can serve two masters. Either he will hate the one and love the other, or he will be devoted to the one and despise the other. You cannot serve both God and Money.

Therefore I tell you, do not worry about your life, what you will eat or drink; or about your body, what you will wear. Is not life more impor-tant than food, and the body more important than clothes? Look at the birds of the air; they do not sow or reap or store away in barns, and yet your heavenly Father feeds them. Are you not much more valuable than they? Who of you by worrying can add a single hour to his life?

And why do you worry about clothes? See how the lilies of the field grow. They do not labor or spin. Yet I tell you that not even Solomon in all his splendor was dressed like one of these. If that is how God clothes the grass of the field, which is here today and tomorrow is thrown into the fire, will he not much more clothe you, O you of little faith? So do not worry saying, "What shall we eat?" or "What shall we drink?" or "What shall we wear?" For the pagans run after all these things, and your heavenly Father knows that you need them. But seek first his kingdom and his righteousness, and all these things will be giv-en to you as well. Therefore do not worry about tomorrow, for tomor-row will worry about itself. Each day has enough trouble of its own.

Introduction

There are three things governing the success of our lives. These three things are far more important than money. In many re-spects these three things actually govern our use or abuse of our fi-nancial resources.

1. Our attitude in life determines our success in life. If we have the right concept of ourselves and other people, we will succeed. It is imperative that we also have the right attitude about material things in the concept of our mission in life. It is not wrong to possess riches and the symbols of wealth so long as they do not possess us. Stewardship is not simply giving money to God out of guilt or with a view of getting money back. We must give with a right attitude, which is the love and adoration for our Heavenly Father.

2. **Relationships also determine personal success in life.** If we are to have a meaningful life, we must have the ability to get along with people. We must know how to develop deep and meaningful relationships regardless of how smart or how gifted we are. If we do not have the ability to establish relationships, we will not be successful in life. We may amass riches, yet we are poor if we do not have the riches of true friends and close families. Relationships are the real measure of the wealth we have. This means that wealth is not measured by a bank balance or a year-end profit and loss statement. Wealth is measured by the richness of our character and that of those who call us their friends. The kind of relationship we have among our friends, associates, and neighbors reveals volumes about our stewardship of the financial resources at our disposal.

3. **Personal priorities in life may be the greatest of the three factors.** When we have priorities we also have objectives. We know what we want in life based on what we believe is really important, and set our objectives. Without priorities we could work hard all of our lives but never accomplish much. To be a success in life we must know what is important and what will give us the greatest return on our investments. Without priorities, work becomes meaningless and life empty. When we know our priorities and work toward them, we can have meaning and fulfillment in life.

Planning Our Priorities

Not long ago, one of America's most renowned newspaper publishers closed its doors. A TV commentator interviewed one of their Pulitzer prize award winning journalists and simply asked, "Why?" The journalist responded, "We forgot our purpose." When their priority to news reporting began to be shuffled in the affairs of making money, they lost their purpose of existence and eventually passed out of existence. Many people could say that about their lives. When Jesus called His disciples together for their first staff meeting, one of the issues He addressed specifically was this area of priorities. He summarized the ultimate priority of every Christian when He said, "Seek first his kingdom and his righteousness and all these things will be given to you" (Matt. 6:33).

In the course of discussing this topic, Jesus suggested several priorities to plan for to determine the real direction of one's life:

1. **What motivates my giving?** The first question Jesus asked involves our attitudes toward money. We can seek the security of money, or we can seek the security of God. The priority in stewardship is seeking first the kingdom of God. There are two things that are implied in this challenge. First, we must know what is important, and second, we must seek what is important. After we have determined what is important, we must seek it. The Greek verb for "seek" (*zeteo*) includes both the ideas of coveting earnestly and striving after something. Only when we have that attitude toward the Kingdom and righteousness of God can we claim the conditional promises of this verse—"all these things will be given to you as well." That means the plan of our lives will fall into place when we seek what is important, then God's provision will be evident.

"But seek first" suggests there are other alternatives. The word "but" indicates there are other options. Jesus realized that some of us will not seek the kingdom of God but will seek another option to God's plan. Another option is seeking to save money. These are treasures we consider important because we put them away in special places. God gives us an option. We can store up for ourselves treasure on earth, or we can seek God's plan. When we seek earthly treasures, there is the possibility of someone breaking in and stealing them. The other option is to lay up treasures in heaven. There thieves cannot break in, nor can we lose our treasures.

"Where your treasure is, there your heart will be also" (Matt. 6:21). Our money reveals our hearts. Jesus was saying, "Show me your treasure, and I will show you your heart." Our check stubs and our credit card bills tell us what is important to us. Often we try to determine our spirituality by our prayer lives or Bible reading, but our check stubs are a more accurate barometer of what is really important to us.

2. **What motivates my direction?** "What am I looking for?" is the real question. Just as a burglar never finds a police officer and boys cutting school never find a teacher, so those of us who refuse to submit to the Lordship of Christ never "find" His blessings. Jesus also asks if we are living for things that will last or for things that will slip away. He indicates our sight is imperative regarding money. "The eye is the lamp of the body. If your eyes are good, your whole

body will be full of light" (Matt. 6:22). Our priorities are evident in the focus of God's Word. If we have the correct view of what is really important in life, everything else falls into order.

3. **What motivates my life?** Jesus said it is impossible to serve two masters. When we try to serve two masters, we will be stretched, divided, and absolutely ineffective. People can tell what we live for by who we serve. In order to make ends meet today, many people try working two jobs for two different companies. Some people have been successful in moonlighting by carefully planning their appointments in life on a precise timetable. But no matter how hard we try, we Christians are not able to moonlight by serving God on one shift and wealth on another. Even though we might try for a while, the crisis will eventually come when we must decide either to serve God or money.

4. **What will I die for?** Dwight L. Moody once declared that people have not found something worth living for until they have found something worth dying for. Jesus emphasized this truth when He spoke of the stressful lifestyles characteristic of the wrong priorities in life. Particularly, Jesus identified anxiety and stress over such things as life, food, drink, clothing, and unchangeable physical features like height as more characteristic of a non-Christian approach to life.

Jesus was not instructing us to not plan ahead when He said, "Do not worry about your life" (Matt. 6:25). By implication He seems to imply in that context it is right to have a proper concern over some things, a caring and concern characterized by careful forethought and genuine interests.

God created us physically to be able to handle a certain amount of healthy stress, but a stress overload can actually kill. When we are anxious over money, we will eventually die for money. If we live for God's kingdom and righteousness, that becomes the object of our sacrifice. Just as a missionary might have to sacrifice his or her life as a martyr or take the gospel to a primitive, unreached tribe, so God wants us to be a "living sacrifice." This is often much harder. One man learned this truth when he recited a love poem to his wife and concluded the poem with the thought that his love for her was so great he would lay down his life for her. "Oh," his wife sighed, "but will you wash the dishes for me?"

5. **What motivates my desires?** Ultimately the priority of life is evident in the secret longings and deep-seated desires of the heart. The question must be asked, "What are we really longing

for?" That is our real priority in life. As we noted earlier, the word "seek" implies the idea of coveting earnestly and striving after. It is not wrong to have such longings if our desires are governed by the right priority. There is a difference between the things the people of this world long after and that which the Christian should have as a deep-seated desire. When Jesus tells us to seek God's kingdom and righteousness, He does not mean we should do it for a weekend, a month, or even a year. The verb is not an aorist tense verb that would imply seeking once and for all but a tense emphasizing a continuous, unending exercise of seeking.

Producing Our Priorities

We make priority judgments every day of our lives. We make value decisions about everything. We need to seek things that are consistent with our priorities in life—God's kingdom and righteousness.

The above questions reveal the priority of the decisions we make in life. Some of us become mystical when we talk about seeking God. When we do we show our lack of knowledge and understanding. We seem to arrive at decisions totally unrelated to the real issues of life, but seeking God is not some mystical discipline. It is practical, measurable, and obtainable.

There are three questions we need to ask concerning the priority decisions in our lives. Answering these questions can help ensure that our major decisions in life are consistent with our predetermined priority of seeking the kingdom and righteousness of God.

1. What will we endure? When we make decisions, many of them have eternal consequences. Therefore we should make decisions that will endure for eternity. Jesus described two kinds of people. The first put their value on this earth, and the other put their value on heaven. If we are in the group that puts value on this earth, we store up things, while those of us who put the most value on eternal perspectives realize that things will last for eternity only if invested in heaven. Therefore, before making major decisions, we should ask ourselves what type of lasting value this decision will give to my family, to my church, and to myself.

2. What will shine? This question asks what will help? Will my decision elevate people? Will the result be positive? Will I be a better person? Will my family be better? We should always ask if a decision has a positive light and if it will help guide in the way of righteousness. Most of our major decisions will have an impact on the lives of others. Consequently, we should make the kinds of decisions that have a positive impact rather than a destructive influence. My decision should follow the guideline of Matt. 5:16, "In the same way, let your light shine before men, that they may see your good deeds and praise your Father in heaven."

3. What will strengthen my faith? We should also ask if a decision is made in faith, realizing it is not faith in ourselves but faith in God. Jesus described His listeners, "O you of little faith" (Matt. 6:30). The phrase "little faith" was used by Jesus to describe His disciples. They could be characterized as having faith in doubt. The disciples were making their decisions outside of faith. While they trusted God to save them for all eternity, they tended to doubt that God was able to provide for their basic needs. The Bible teaches that God is both able to save our souls for eternity and to supply our needs while we are here on this earth. If God takes care of the birds and the lilies, He will most certainly take care of us.

Conclusion

Some Christians have developed an erroneous view of the Christian life that views Christ as a kind of glorified Santa Claus. They believe they can childishly sit back and make demands from God without accepting personal responsibility or even having right priorities in life.

We have no legitimate right to claim a promise from God until we have done our part in meeting the conditions associated with the particular promises. We are to come to God and seek His kingdom and His righteousness. Jesus modeled this principle when He humbled himself and left the glory that was rightfully His to become a man and provide for our salvation. Because Jesus sought first the Kingdom and righteousness, God rewarded Him by restoring Him to His original glory and greatly elevating His name.

When we settle the priority issue in life, we will adopt the attitude of Christ concerning stewardship. Only then will we understand the wisdom of Jim Elliot who, as a college student, penned the words, "He is no fool who gives what he cannot keep to gain what he cannot lose."

Developing Responsible Stewards

Luke 19:11-27

While they were listening to this, he went on to tell them a parable, because he was near Jerusalem and the people thought that the kingdom of God was going to appear at once. He said, "A man of noble birth went to a distant country to have himself appointed king and then to return. So he called ten of his servants and gave them ten minas. 'Put this money to work,' he said, 'until I come back.'

"But his subjects hated him and sent a delegation after him to say, 'We don't want this man to be our king.'

"He was made king, however, and returned home. Then he sent for the servants to whom he had given the money, in order to find out what they had gained with it.

"The first one came and said, 'Sir, your mina has earned ten more.'

"'Well done, my good servant!' his master replied. 'Because you have been trustworthy in a very small matter, take charge of ten cities.'

"The second came and said, 'Sir, your mina has earned five more.'

"His master answered, 'You take charge of five cities.'

"Then another servant came and said, 'Sir, here is your mina; I have kept it laid away in piece of cloth. I was afraid of you, because you are a hard man. You take out what you did not put in and reap what you did not sow.'

"His master replied, 'I will judge you by your own words, you wicked servant! You knew, did you, that I am a hard man, taking out what I did not put in, and reaping what I did not sow? Why then didn't you put my money on deposit, so that when I came back, I could have collected it with interest?'

"Then he said to those standing by, 'Take his mina away from him and give it to the one who has ten minas.'

"'Sir,' they said, 'he already has ten!'

"He replied, 'I tell you that to everyone who has, more will be given, but as for the one who has nothing, even what he has will be taken away. But those enemies of mine who did not want me to be king over them—bring them here and kill them in front of me.'"

Introduction

For years an army recruitment advertisement has been challenging young men and women to "Be all that you can be." As a Christian the challenge should be, "Be all God meant you to be."

Although these catchy phrases are not found in biblical text, they certainly express foundational truth. God desires that each of us develop all of our potential for His glory and His honor. Jesus gave us several parables emphasizing this very principle. Just before His journey to Calvary, Jesus told the story of a certain nobleman who received a kingdom. Later He repeated a similar story emphasizing several similar principles. While these stories were different, even a casual reading of both of them will reveal several similarities. In both cases, a master entrusted his wealth to his servants while he was away from his estate. In both cases they were servants with some degree of success in investing their masters' wealth and turning a profit.

Both stories record the example of a servant who, for some reason, had not wisely invested his master's money and, as a result, had no profit to report. In both cases the unfaithful servant fell into immediate disfavor with the master. The fact that Jesus would teach two similar stories within the period of about a week so close to His crucifixion only serves to emphasize how important He thought the principles of these parables were.

Developing Principle-Driven Stewards

This parable teaches that everyone has a responsibility to God even when we only have a little that is committed to us. The Greek word *mna,* translated "mina" ("pound" in KJV) in this parable, refers to a sum of 100 denarii, worth about $16.00. In terms of the economy of that day, it was worth almost a third of the annual wage of the common laborer. In a culture of extreme wealth and extreme poverty, one mina would probably have not impressed the major traders and bankers of the day. Even though the amount was not significant, the servants were each responsible to their master and ultimately accountable for what they did with their resources. The concern of God is not how much we have but how faithful we are. Even though different servants produced different results, Jesus was pleased with the degree of success each had experienced. His great disappointment, however, was not how little a person produced. He was disappointed with the person who did nothing at all with the trust he had received. The master expected him to use that money in an effective way just as God wants us to maximize our effective use of the various resources He grants us. Responsibility leads to accountability, and we will someday each be accountable for our stewardship.

Principles That Drive Stewardship

1. **The master will return.** In this parable, the master was pictured as one who would return. The master had no apparent communication with his servants while he was away. He did not ask for regular reports. There seemed to be no communication at all. The workers had their instructions and their responsibility. While there was no weekly evaluation by the master, the day finally arrived when the master did return and the accountability report was required.

The foundation of stewardship is clear. We will give an account when the Lord returns and asks for it. Jesus said, "And if I go to prepare a place for you, I will come back" (John 14:3). When the Lord returns, we will be accountable for the gifts He has given to us. We will not be accountable for someone else's gifts, nor for what others have given to us. We will only be responsible for what God has given to us.

2. **Jesus believes in us.** Because Jesus believes in us, He gives us His possessions. The servants were told, "Put this money to work . . . until I come back" (Luke 19:13). The Greek verb *pragmateuomai,* translated "occupy," is a commercial term meaning "trade." Clearly the master intended his servants to invest wisely so that the master's holdings would increase.

The work of the Kingdom is so great that many wonder why God left it to us. If most of us had an important task, we probably would not give it to another person; we would do it ourselves. But God has given us the most important task in the world. He told us to go and teach and advance His kingdom. He challenged us to be salt and light in society. Even though this is a great task, He is not going to do it by himself. God chooses and wants to work through us and with us and in the final analysis, He wants us to fulfill the task for Him. We would not trust other people with a task so awesome, but God believes in us.

3. **Judgment Day will come.** When the master returned, he only had one question . . . "What have you done with what I gave you?" Although he, like most businessmen, was concerned with the bottom line on the profit and loss statement, he did not outwardly appear upset with the amount of the return. He was primarily focused on how his servants used what was given to them. The greatest judgment was for the one who did not do anything with what was given to him. Because God works in us and with us, it is impossible to use a gift that God has given to us and not have a good

return with it. In God's kingdom, He gives us more responsibility when we demonstrate our faithfulness. When we do our work faithfully, He rewards us with greater responsibility.

Developing Proper Stewardship Attitudes

The attitudes reflected by the individuals in these two parables are characteristic of attitudes common in the world of our churches today. If we are going to be responsible with the resources God has placed at our disposal, it is important that we understand these attitudes as we evaluate our own attitudes toward stewardship.

First attitude: **What's God's is mine, and I'm going to take it.**

If we have this attitude, we want the possessions, the blessings, and the resources of the Lord, but we don't want God to reign over us. We want life on our own terms, and sometimes we are aggressive in this attitude. We try to live by our own rules. This attitude will make us inward focused. It is a worldly attitude. Because the world wants the latest gadgets, they respect the people who have them. However, in the worldly appetite of possession of things, people are never satisfied. Those in this category will never have enough of anything.

Second attitude: **What's mine is mine, and I'm going to keep it.**

With this attitude we would not steal from God. We would not want to take from others. We would just want what we felt was ours. We will not be guilty of taking away or destroying anything, but we will also not be involved in building or developing anything with God's resources either. We fail to recognize that we benefit to some degree from the long-term investment of others and in that sense have the responsibility to consider the needs of future generations. Those of us who have this attitude never ask the important questions, nor are we part of the process of life. We forget that our responsibility is to leave life better for the next generation than we found it.

Third attitude (the proper attitude): **What's mine is God's, and He can have it.**

When we have this attitude, we realize that everything we have belongs to God. We know God will get it whether or not we give it. We realize that we are stewards of what God has given to us, and we understand the responsibilities of our stewardship. We become givers of life; we are not takers, nor are we selfish.

Conclusion

A man moved to New England and was building a house. He didn't know where to dig his well, so he allowed an old-timer to find water with the divining stick. The stick seems to bend where there is an underground river running near the surface. The old-timer said to the new resident, "You must pump the water each day." As he left, again he warned the resident, "Pump the water each day."

At the beginning, the new resident pumped water from the well each day and found that the water in the well got sweeter. The more water he pumped, the more water there seemed to be. After a period of time, the new owner forgot about pumping the well and went on a trip. When he came back, there was still water in the well. However, it only lasted two days and then the well went dry. The next time he went to town, he told the old-timer about his dry well. "Did you pump the water every day?" the old-timer asked. He explained that an underground river is fed by thousands of capillaries. As water flows through these capillaries, the power of the river keeps them open, but when the water is not pumped out of the well, the river becomes stagnant and the capillaries fill, resulting in the river seeking another route through the underground. "You lost the river," the old-timer explained, "because you quit using the water." It is the same with God.

Christians must take from God. The more we claim from God, the more He will give in return. Our wealth is like the water in an underground river. The more we pump our wealth into the work of God, the more God replenishes it for His service. We must pump our wealth continually into the work of God to advance His kingdom.

Some Christians lament the fact that something is missing in their spiritual lives. It seems that the joy and enthusiasm that was once a part of serving Jesus is gone and the Christian life has almost become an endurance test. However, when we fail to use the resources God has given to us, our spiritual wealth dries up. We don't need more spiritual food in the Christian community today. What we need is more exercise. We need to remember that someday Jesus is coming back, and when He comes, He is going to ask one question, "What have you done with what I gave you?"

Developing Committed Stewards

Matt. 21:33-43

"Listen to another parable. There was a landowner who planted a vineyard. He put a wall around it, dug a winepress in it and built a watchtower. Then he rented the vineyard to some farmers and went away on a journey. When the harvest time approached he sent his servants to the tenants to collect his fruit.

"The tenants seized his servants; they beat one, killed another, and stoned a third. Then he sent other servants to them, more than the first time, and the tenants treated them the same way. Last of all, he sent his son to them. 'They will respect my son,' he said.

"But when the tenants saw the son, they said to each other, 'This is the heir. Come, let's kill him and take his inheritance.' So they took him and threw him out of the vineyard and killed him.

"Therefore, when the owner of the vineyard comes, what will he do to those tenants?"

"He will bring those wretches to a wretched end," they replied, "and he will rent the vineyard to other tenants, who will give him his share of the crop at harvest time."

Jesus said to them, "Have you never read in the Scriptures: 'The stone the builders rejected has become the capstone; the Lord has done this, and it is marvelous in our eyes'?

"Therefore I tell you that the kingdom of God will be taken away from you and given to a people who will produce its fruit."

Introduction

It was March 30, 1975. Most people assumed Bertha Adams was just another welfare victim, but an autopsy revealed that she had severe malnutrition and evidences of poverty were abundant in her apartment . . . the lack of heat, the lack of food, the lack of basic necessities of life. There could only be one conclusion . . . Bertha Adams was an obvious example of one who was missed by the national safety net of social spending. Then there came the surprise. While taking inventory of her personal effects, authorities found two keys. They trusted a hunch and took the keys to a neighborhood bank. There they found a safety deposit box. In that safety deposit box they found $799,000 in cash. Also stuffed into this box were hundreds of valuable and negotiable stock certificates, bonds, and other securities. Mrs. Adams had a misguided perspective when it came to stewardship. In her view, her possessions were something to be hoarded. She did not understand that the blessings of God were given to her to be used to meet the needs not only of herself but also of others. She didn't understand that the purpose of life was to manage her resources and not selfishly clutch them for herself.

The Christian is the steward of all the resources God has given, including time, talent, and treasure. The faithful steward manages all resources for the glory of God. Yet, tragically, there are many Christians who have misunderstood stewardship and are poor managers of the resources of God under their control. Let's look at misguided perspectives of stewardship.

Stewardship Is Fund-raising

First, there is the wrong idea that **stewardship is fund-raising**. Many often think that a stewardship program in the local church is raising money much as community agencies raise money. Even though the money is raised for the church budget, that should never be the bottom line. Stewardship initiative should teach church members how God wants them to spend their money. When Christians realize that all of their money belongs to God, not just the tithe, they will spend their money as stewards for God. Stewards are not hoarders of money but are money-managers. When Christians are properly taught, they will not only give liberally to God but also spend the remaining funds according to God's plan. As a result, the Kingdom will prosper and church giving will continue to grow.

The Giving Perspective

Another misguided perspective of stewardship is **the giving perspective**. Many Christians think that stewardship is giving money rather than managing our assets for God. We only can give what we own. If we realize that we do not own something in the first place, it is much easier for us to give it back to God. We do not own our money; we do not own our possessions, even the clothes on our back, for everything belongs to God. For example, if we drive a company car downtown, we know that it is not our car. We are only using it for a stated purpose and that is for the business. That is how we should treat our possessions. God is letting us use our money for His business. Therefore, if we are involved in a stewardship campaign or a stewardship program, it should be only to educate the church members in the use of our time, talent, and treasures for the glory of God.

The Permanent Possession Perspective

A third misguided perspective of stewardship is **the permanent possession perspective.** We think humanly that we can keep things indefinitely. Though we all know we can't take it with us, we often think we are the exception. The Bible teaches us that we leave this world as naked as we entered it. We often think that somehow we can escape this law. Functionally we think of things as permanent rather than temporary. If we are confused and frustrated in our stewardship of financial resources, it may be because we see them primarily as permanent personal assets that someone is trying to take away from us. When we view stewardship as the management of God's resources rather than permanent personal ownership, we take the "stew" out of stewardship.

Motivating Principles of Stewardship

Jesus described a landowner who found and purchased a field, tilled the soil, planted a vineyard, planted a thick hedge about its perimeter, and dug wells to irrigate the vineyard. The vineyard was equipped with a tower that not only provided housing for the workers but also was part of the security system designed to protect the vineyard from thieves and wild animals. He did everything to make the vineyard productive, then committed it to its workers. They were to produce a crop and pay him rent in the form of some portion of the crop. The owner then left the vineyard and went away.

The story of Jesus could have been about any one of the hundreds of vineyards scattered throughout Palestine in His day. It was common for wealthy people to purchase and build well-equipped vineyards, then rent them out to the tenant farmers. Because of the civil unrest in Judea at that time, most wealthy Greek or Roman landlords preferred to live elsewhere and viewed property in Judea as income property. As in most of the parables of Jesus, there was nothing foreign to the setting of this parable that His listeners would have had difficulty understanding. Actually, the parable may be as much based on the Old Testament as on the New Testament. In the Old Testament, Israel was described as the "vineyard of God." The context of Jesus' parable was obvious to the chief priests and Pharisees who first heard the story. They knew this simple story had specific application to the nation of Israel and her response to the servants of the Son of God. They realized Jesus was accusing them of being poor stewards or managers of Israel and the vineyard of God. In the parable Jesus reminded the Jewish leaders of several important stewardship principles. The principles apply as much today as they did when Jesus gave the parable.

1. **The principle of blessing.** In this parable the landowner saw to it that the vineyard was completely equipped, lacking nothing necessary to run the business of the vineyard efficiently. Like every vineyard in Palestine, this one was equipped with a winepress probably carved out of a solid rock, although occasionally these were made with bricks. The tower provided housing for the workers and also served as a watchtower where a worker could ensure that the vineyard was protected. The fence around the vineyard was probably a thick, thorny hedge that would discourage the wild animals that might damage or destroy the vineyard. The owner expected the workers to manage the vineyard for him. As Christians today, we are similar to the workers and God is the owner. Our responsibility is to manage the vineyard for Him. Everything in this world belongs to God, who created it and has redeemed it for himself. He not only owns the resources in the world but also gives us good minds, good health, circumstances to get an education, and even initiative to provide for our families. We do not own the things around us. We are not even owners of our health or desires. God and God alone has given us everything, and He expects us to use these things for His glory.

The psalmist recognized the source of all his benefits and responded, "I praise you because I am fearfully and wonderfully made; your works are wonderful, I know that full well" (Ps. 139:14).

When we consider all the things with which God has blessed us, it is sometimes almost embarrassing to see how little we have done with it. Perhaps, quite possibly the greatest waste in the world is to have the potential God has given us and do nothing with it. A good steward will always manage these resources for the Kingdom's best interests.

2. **The principle of revelation.** When the owner is out of sight, he is usually out of mind. The parable indicates that the landowner committed his vineyard to the workers and went into a "far country." Absentee landlords were very popular in Palestine because the area had a lot of civil unrest and lacked the luxuries common in oth-

er parts of the Roman Empire. These workers were not different from most people. When we are not around people, we tend to forget the important things, like birthdays and the things that are important to them. The longer the owner is gone, the less we see of him and the more we forget about him. We forget that God has given us everything. Some of us realize that God has given us families and homes and jobs and cars and furniture—the blessings of life. But after we work hard for a promotion or another thing, we could at times begin to think that we have attained these things by our own talents and our own abilities. The longer we see the things that God has given us without recognizing His ownership, the more likely we are to begin to see them as our own. We forget that God is the owner and has allowed us and given us all that we have.

3. **The principle of belief.** The owner of the vineyard had the incredible belief in his employees that they would bring a return on his investment. First, he gave control over his resources. Further, he expected their full cooperation. Finally, he refused to believe his workers were in revolt against him. The owner kept sending people back to collect on his investment. The workers beat the first one, killed the second, and stoned the third. When additional servants were sent out by the owner, they met with the same fate. The owner continued to think the best of the tenants and sent his own son, whom they also killed. Until this point in the story, everything has been very credible. Here, however, the actions of the landlord were most unusual. Many commentators have observed that no person would send his son into a situation where the servants had been repeatedly abused and killed. The natural response of the landowner under such circumstances would be to send in the authorities to deal with the delinquent tenants. The contrast here is between what man would do and what God has already done.

God did send His Son to a nation that consistently rejected the prophets and ultimately rejected His Son. But, the application goes far beyond the Jewish nation. Paul reminded a predominantly Gentile church, "But God demonstrates his own love for us in this: While we were still sinners, Christ died for us" (Rom. 5:8). God loves us so much that even when we hoard or try to keep what belongs to Him, He continues to give us another chance. He is always the God of a second chance.

4. **The principle of judgment.** We realize that we are accountable to God for what He has given to us. We are not accountable for what we don't have, only for what is committed to us to manage as

stewards. A day is coming when every one of us will give an account of our stewardship to God. The parable tells us, "Therefore, when the owner of the vineyard comes, what will he do to those tenants?" (Matt. 21:40). If God has given to us resources to manage, then a day is coming when we must give an account to Him. Everyone is accountable to God, and the day of reckoning or the Day of Judgment is sure.

Conclusion

In the days of the American Revolution there lived in Ephrata, Pennsylvania, a Baptist pastor by the name of Peter Miller. He was a man who enjoyed the friendship of George Washington. In the same city lived another man, named Michael Whitman, an ungodly scoundrel who did everything in his power to obstruct and oppose the work of the pastor. On one occasion, Michael Whitman was involved in an act of treason against the government of the United States. He was arrested and taken to Philadelphia, 70 miles away, to appear before General Washington. When the news reached Peter Miller that this man, his enemy, was appearing on trial for his life before General Washington, Peter Miller walked the 70 miles to Philadelphia to appeal for the life of this man. He was admitted to the presence of General Washington because of his friendship. When he entered the hearing room, he began without delay to speak for the life of Michael Whitman. Washington listened to him and heard his story through, then said, "No, Peter, I cannot give you the life of your friend." Peter Miller said, "My friend! My friend! This man is not my friend. He is the bitterest enemy I have." Washington said, "What? You mean to say that you have walked 70 miles through the dust and the heat of the road to appeal for the life of your enemy? Well, that puts this matter in a different light. I will give you, then, the life of your enemy." Peter Miller put his arm around the shoulders of Michael Whitman and led him out of the very shadow of death back to his own home, no longer his enemy but a friend.

This is what the Lord Jesus has done for us continually. When we were enemies, when we were yet without strength, when we were helpless, when we were opposed to God, fighting Him every way we could, rebelling again His precepts and principles, leading self-centered lives without regard for His rights, using His goods and His resources, Christ Jesus died for us. That is the beauty of stewardship. That is the beauty of giving.

STEWARDSHIP
STORIES

George Burns has given an entertainer's perspective on stewardship: "It's easier to make a paying audience laugh. They get dressed and they put on a tie and they get in their cars and they pay so much that they like your act. An audience that doesn't pay is very critical." He's right! Critical church members seldom have many check stubs that bear the church's name.

The late Queen Mary was walking in the vicinity of Balmoral on a dark and cloudy day. She strolled rather far, and as the rain came down she stopped at a cottage to borrow an umbrella. The woman did not recognize the queen, so decided to give the stranger an old umbrella with a broken rib. The next morning a man in gold braid appeared at the cottage door. "The Queen asked me to thank you for lending her the umbrella," he explained. The woman in the cottage was dumbfounded and with tears flowing down her checks said, "What an opportunity I missed! Why did I not give the Queen the best umbrella I had?"

—Adapted from A. Naismith, *1,200 Notes, Quotes, and Anecdotes* (London, 1962), 81.

Dr. G. Campbell Morgan recalls that when the Salvation Army started its work, General William Booth was charged with dishonesty. People said that all the property was in his name and that he at any time might have converted that property into money and appropriated it for himself. That was the criticism of the work. However, from the very first, he was careful to publish his accounts, and in the process of the years that criticism ceased entirely.

—G. Campbell Morgan, *The Corinthian Letters of Paul* (Old Tappan, N.J.: Fleming H. Revell Co., 1946), 253.

Dr. Billy Graham has been accused of conducting his crusades for personal gain, but wisely and scripturally he has seen to it that reputable accountants in each city have made public all facts and figures relating to a crusade. Furthermore, he insists on putting himself on salary, in common with other members of his team. With careful management, over time less and less criticism has

been leveled at this evangelist whom God has used so greatly. Many other instances could be cited to illustrate this basic principle of the church of "providing honorable things, not only in the sight of the Lord, but also in the sight of men."

At a church meeting, a very wealthy man rose to tell the rest of those present about his Christian faith. "I'm a millionaire," he said, "and I attribute it all to the rich blessings of God in my life. I remember that turning point in my faith. I had just earned my first dollar, and I went to a church meeting that night. The speaker was a missionary who told about his work. I knew that I only had a dollar bill and had to either give it all to God's work or nothing at all. So at that moment I decided to give my whole dollar to God. I believe that God blessed that decision, and that is why I am a rich man today."

He finished and there was an awed silence at his testimony as he moved toward his seat. As he sat down a little old lady sitting in the same pew leaned over and said to him: "I dare you to do it again."

There was a knock on the door of the hut occupied by a missionary in Africa. Answering, the missionary found one of the native boys holding a large fish in his hands. The boy said, "Reverend, you taught us what tithing is, so here—I've brought you my tithe." As the missionary gratefully took the fish, he questioned the young lad, "If this is your tithe, where are the other nine fish?" At this, the boy beamed and said, "Oh, they're still back in the river. I'm going to catch them now."

One Sunday morning the pastor encouraged his congregation to consider the potential of the church. He told them, "With God's help we can see the day when this church will go from crawling to walking."

The people responded, "Let the church walk, Pastor. Let the church walk."

He continued, "And when the church begins to walk, next the church can begin to run."

And the people shouted, "Let the church run, Pastor. Let the church run!"

The pastor continued, "And finally the church can move from running to flying. Oh, the church can fly! But, of course, that's going to take lots of money for that to happen."

The congregation grew quiet and from the back someone mumbled, "Let the church crawl, Pastor. Let the church crawl."

I read of one pastor who perceived the whole concept of encouragement from a financial point of view. He announced one Sunday that he had made a new offering box for the weekly collection of the tithes and offering. He claimed that it was designed to encourage people to become better stewards of their money.

"This new box," he explained, "has some interesting features. When you drop in a check or paper money in large amounts, the box makes no sound at all. Put a quarter in, and it tinkles like a bell. A dime blows a whistle, and a penny fires a shot. When you put in nothing, the box takes your picture."

A priest once asked one of his parishioners to serve as financial chairman of his parish. The man, manager of a grain elevator, agreed on two conditions: No report would be due for a year, and no one would ask any questions during the year.

At the end of the church year he made his report. He had paid off the church debt of $200,000. He had redecorated the church. He had sent $1,000 to missions. He had $5,000 in the bank.

"How did you do all this?" asked the priest and the shocked congregation.

Quietly he answered, "You people bring your grain to my elevator. As you did business with me, I simply withheld 10 percent and gave it to the church. You never missed it."

He was not too well-educated and his manner was somewhat crude and rough, but he became a Christian and was on fire for the Lord. He constantly pestered his pastor to help him be of some genuine service to his church. In desperation, the pastor gave him a list of 10 people, saying, "These are members who seldom attend services; some are prominent men of the city. Contact them any way you can and try to get them to be more faithful. Use the church stationery to write letters if you want, but get them back in church." He accepted the challenge with enthusiasm. About three weeks later, a letter arrived from a prominent physician, whose name was on the list. In the envelope was a thousand dollar check and a note: "Dear Pastor: Enclosed is my check to make up for my missed offerings. I'm sorry for missing worship so much, but be assured I am going to be present every Sunday from now on and will not by choice miss any services again. Sincerely, M. B. Jones, M.D. P.S. Would you kindly tell your secretary that there is only one *t* in *dirty* and no *c* in *skunk*."

The pastor got up at the beginning of a huge stewardship rally, held his hands up for silence, and said, "Friends, I have a marvelous announcement to make about our building fund and our stewardship program for the coming year." He paused for the import of his opening remark to sink in. He then added with dramatic phrasing, "Friends, we have the money!" A buzz of excitement went through the congregation. He held up his hands for quiet once again. He finished, "Yes, we have all the money we need. Now all we have to do is give it."

Dr. Hugh McKean of Chiengmai, Thailand, tells of a church of 400 members where every member tithes. They receive a weekly wage of 40 stangs (less than 20 cents) and their rice. Of this meager existence, each gives a tenth each week. Because of this, they have done more for Christ in Thailand than any other church. They pay their own preacher and have sent two missionary families to spread the gospel in a community cut off from the outside world. They are intensely interested in all forms of Christian work, especially work for unfortunates of every kind; and their gifts for this kind of work are large. They have not only accepted Christ but, having found Him good, are making Him known to others. Oh, by the way, this church of tithers is also a church of lepers—every person has leprosy.

A church member was having trouble with the concept of tithing. One day he revealed his doubts to his minister. "Pastor, I just don't see how I can give 10 percent of my income to the church when I can't even keep on top of our bills."

The pastor replied, "John, if I promise to make up the difference in your bills if you fall short, do you think you could try tithing for just one month?"

After a moment's pause, John responded, "Sure, if you promise to make up any shortage, I guess I could try tithing for one month."

"Now, what do you think of that," mused the pastor. "You say you'd be willing to put your trust in a mere man like myself, who possesses so little materially, but you couldn't trust your Heavenly Father who owns the whole universe!" The next Sunday, John gave his tithe and has been doing so faithfully ever since.

Fifty-seven pennies that were found under a little girl's pillow when she died left their mark on Philadelphia. The girl wanted to enter a little Sunday School in Philadelphia the year before and was told that there was not enough room. She began saving her pennies to "help the Sunday School have more room."

Two years later she became ill and died, and they found a small pocketbook under her pillow with 57 pennies and a piece of paper that had the following note written very neatly: "To help build the Little Temple bigger, so more children can go to Sunday School."

The pastor told the story to his congregation, and the newspaper took the story across the country. Soon the pennies grew, and the outcome can be seen in Philadelphia today. There is a church that will seat 3,300 persons, a Temple University that accommodates thousands of students, a Temple Hospital, and a large Temple Sunday School. And it all began with a beautiful, dedicated spirit—and 57 pennies.

It takes concern, commitment, dedication, and love to give oneself. In the words of Jesus at the conclusion of the parable of the Good Samaritan: "Go, and do thou likewise" (Luke 10:37, KJV).

John Allan Lavender tells the story of a pastor who after making an appeal at his church for Faith Promise, a certain woman, a member of the church, came to him and handed him a check for

$50, asking at the same time if her gift was satisfactory. The pastor immediately replied, "If it represents you."

There was a moment of soul-searching thought and she asked to have the check returned to her. She left with it and a day or two later she returned handing the pastor a check for $5,000 and again asked the same question, "Is my gift satisfactory?" The pastor gave the same answer as before, "If it represents you." As before, a truth seemed to be driving deeply. After a few moments of hesitation she took back the check and left.

Later in the week she came again with a check. That time it was for $50,000. As she placed it in the pastor's hand, she said, "After earnest, prayerful thought I have come to the conclusion that this gift does represent me, and I am happy to give it."

Perhaps in this light the words from 1 Cor. 16:2, "as God hath prospered him" (KJV), may take on new meaning.

Jack Exum loves to share concerning his trip to Canada. While there he visited a farmer who operated a large grain farm. His spread included some 2,500 acres. I asked him how he planted the seed. He reached in a bin and pulled out an ear of corn. Then he proceeded to pop out the kernels one by one as he walked along, demonstrating the planting process. Do you believe that?

No sir! That's not what he said nor is it what he did. He showed Jack a distributor that was some 30 feet wide. "We take that double tandem truck, fill it with certified seed, back it up to the distributor, open the slots, and pour in the seed." He went on to say, "If you're ever going to be cheap, *don't be cheap with the seed.*"

One bushel of seed invested yields 30 bushels of grain harvested in a good year. Thirty to one—not a bad return, if you are ready to believe and willing to invest. God says, "Believe Me, trust Me, try My plan, prove My ways, and see the kind of harvest I will give." So Paul guarantees this principle of truth in the Scripture with the promise, "And God is able to make all grace abound toward you; that ye, always having all sufficiency in all things, may abound to every good work" (2 Cor. 9:8, KJV).

All grace, all ways, all sufficiency, all things! There are four promises in one breath. Knowing it is one thing, believing it is quite another.

A man called at the church and asked if he could speak to the Head Hog at the Trough. The secretary said, "Who?"

The man replied, "I want to speak to the Head Hog at the Trough!"

Sure now that she had heard correctly, the secretary said, "Sir, if you mean our pastor, you will have to treat him with more respect—and ask for 'The Reverend' or 'The Pastor.' But certainly you cannot refer to him as the Head Hog at the Trough!"

At this, the man came back, "Oh, I see. Well, I have $10,000 I was thinking about donating to the Building Fund."

Secretary: "Hold the line—I think the Big Pig just walked in the door."

The pastor responded to a member: "You say you can't give to the church because you owe everyone. Don't you feel you owe the Lord something?" The member responded, "Yes, of course I do. But He isn't pushing me like the others."

Lawrence L. Durgin wrote: "Christian stewardship is the matching of gift for matchless gift: our life and its whole substance for the gift of perfect love. And though God's Son and His precious death are matchless—in the strange economy of God our gift returned is made sufficient. My all for His all. Stewardship is your commitment: the asking of God to take you back unto Himself—all that you have and all that you are."

—Frank S. Mead, ed. *12,000 Religious Quotations* (Grand Rapids: Baker Book House, 1989), 427.

"Pastor," said a young man, "I am a wild spender. I throw my money around right and left. In this morning's service I want you to pray that I may be cured of this habit."

"Yes, son," agreed the pastor, "the prayer will come right after the offering."

Philip Guedalla, an eminent biographer, declared that the hardest problem the biographer faces is that of discovering the real person about whom he is to write. It is fairly easy, he said, to find out what the subject did, where the subject went, and what the subject said; but what kind of person lives inside is a different matter. Guedalla illustrated his point by citing his biography of the Duke of Wellington. He came across unimpeachable evidence when he discovered Wellington's old checkbooks.

Marcus Bach, longtime professor at the University of Iowa, shared this story. One budget Sunday, a man sat in his usual pew, thinking: *In what way is my life different from that of men who never go to church? What have I ever done that is unusual or startlingly religious?* He couldn't think of a single, solitary instance in which he felt he had distinguished himself as a Christian. He had attended church hundreds of times, but the services had never really taken hold of him. He recalled struggles, sacrifices, gambles in his business, but he could not recall a single gamble for God! While in this mood, he noticed a blank pledge card in the pew rack before him. He picked it up, fingered it, then wrote $5,000 and dropped it in the offering plate.

That afternoon there was a knock at the layman's door. Pledge card in hand, there stood the minister, who had been told to clarify the pledge. He asked, hesitatingly, "Tell me, what's the meaning of this? Do you mean $50, or maybe $500? It says *$5,000!*"

Some years ago, a 94-year-old widow died in her home in Chicago. She was known as a collector of antiques. The administrator of her estate found an astonishing collection of things. There was a 50-year-old collection of chinaware, paintings, and unopened trunks. It was reported that altogether there were 20 rooms packed with rare and expensive furnishings. A fortune in diamonds was found in the false bottom of an old trunk. A desk revealed $5,000 in cash, as well as many uncashed checks and money orders. Some of the checks were so old they were worthless, and many of the money orders were sent to Washington for redemption. What would you have done with such a vast fortune? Do you think the poor, rich woman knew what life was all about?

Like the eccentric lady in Chicago, we, too, are connoisseurs of what we term valuables, yet fail to use them properly, leaving the gifts and promises of God unclaimed.

A national survey, conducted by scientists at the Alcohol, Drug Abuse, and Mental Health Administration, found that over half of Americans feel at least moderate stress in their lives. What is surprising is that the more highly paid and educated report higher and more persistent levels of stress. Apparently, education may lead to a higher income but not necessarily to a higher life. Indeed, stress soared with the level of income, a factor many economically pressed citizens can hardly understand. And, more bad news, those who can most afford to enjoy the high life often don't, missing meals and sleep, drinking more often, and getting less exercise. Perhaps even more unexpected, women, usually considered more tolerant of difficult situations, suffer more stress than men.

It seems that money becomes so important to people that all other aspects of life become secondary. When that happens, wealth becomes a vicious deity, inflicting an equally vicious penalty. Anticipating the problem from the first, God explained how we could have peace with Him and financial security. God clothed Adam and Eve with skins, undoubtedly from the animal he sacrificed as an offering for their sins. God was teaching a lesson: He will be faithful to our needs if we are faithful to His forgiveness.

A former city employee mailed Frank J. O'Brien, city treasurer of Albany, New York, a $100 bill marked "money for stolen time."

We are stewards of our time as much as we are stewards of our money. We are going to give an account of our moments as well as of our words. One of the most terrible thoughts ever devised by man is that which is inherent in the common phrase that this or that occupation is engaged in as a "pastime." Usage may have dropped the second "s" from the spelling, but the idea is that we must find something to pass the time away. May God help us to change our thinking that the idea of "pass time" is to "steal time." That is more true, and in stealing it, we rob both ourselves and God.

An IRS auditor tells the story of a man with an income under $5,000 who claimed he gave $624 to his church. "Sure, he was within the 20 percent limit," the agent said, "but it looked mighty suspicious to me. So I dropped in on the guy and asked him about his return. I thought he would become nervous like most of them do, but not this guy."

"Have you a receipt from the church?" I asked, figuring that would make him squirm. "Sure," he replied, "I always drop them in the drawer." And off he went to get his checks and receipts.

Well, he had me. One look and I knew he was on the level. I apologized for bothering him, explaining that I have to check on deductions that seem unusually high. As I was leaving he invited me to attend his church. "Thanks, I belong to a church myself." "Excuse me," he replied, "that possibility never occurred to me."

As I drove home, I kept wondering what he meant by that last remark. It wasn't until Sunday morning when I put my usual dollar in the offering plate that it came to me.

STEWARDSHIP
QUOTES

It's not how much of my money will I give to God, but how much of God's money will I keep for myself.　　—Oswald Smith

It is in giving that we receive. . . . It is in dying that we are born to eternal life.　　—Francis of Assisi

Giving needs no more apology than does praying. In the Bible there are 1,539 passages that reference giving, while there are only 523 that refer to praying!

When a man is rich, God gets a partner or the man loses his soul.　　—Anonymous

Stewardship is the acceptance from God of personal responsibility for all of life and life's affairs.

There is no portion of our time that is our time, and the rest God's; there is no portion of money that is our money and the rest God's money. It is all His; He made it all, gives it all, and He simply trusted it to us for His service.

Stewardship is what a man does after he says "I believe."

—W. H. Greener

The two things that, of all others, most want to be under a strict rule, and which are the greatest blessings to ourselves and to others, when they are rightly used, are our time and our money.

Entirely too much has been said in most churches about the stewardship of money and too little about the stewardship of power. The modern equivalent of repentance is the responsible use of power.

>——<

Nothing that is God's is obtainable by money.

>——<

Make all you can, save all you can, give all you can.

—John Wesley

>——<

Heroic giving means glorious blessing.   —P. F. Bresee

>——<

I will give all that I have and trust the Lord for the rest.

—P. F. Bresee

>——<

It is one of the peculiarities of holy people, they pay well as well as pray and testify well.   —P. F. Bresee

>——<

There is that which we hold in our hands, of possessions and influence, which are to be no longer held as unto ourselves or so as to revolve around ourselves; they are to be melted into our life's devotement unto Jesus Christ.   —P. F. Bresee

>——<

The smallest gift that means sacrifice means more than the larger gift that does not.

>——<

How may we waste the Lord's goods? Using them for unnecessary display or luxury. Making unnecessary provision for old age. Making unnecessary provision for heirs.

To rob God is to rob ourselves.

Whatever possessions the Lord puts in our hands, we are to hold for Him and use unto Him. Great and prayerful care should be taken in reference to the investment of the Lord's money He has entrusted to our care.

It is right to want what we need, it is praiseworthy to want what is necessary to do the Lord's work.

He who is not liberal with what he has does not deceive himself when he thinks he would be liberal if he had more.

Maybe we were better off when charity was a virtue instead of a deduction.

No person was ever honored for what he received. Honor has been the reward for what he gave.　　　　　—Calvin Coolidge

In Revelation, we read of a book which no man could open. Some believe that was the pocketbook.　　　　　—Anonymous

People no longer give to the church simply because it is the church. The church must prove it is worthy of donations through the mark it leaves on the world.

God is the owner and giver of all, we are His stewards.

　　　　　—C. Neil Strait

Generous giving produces rejoicing in one's soul.

—David M. Vaughn

When it comes to giving, some folks stop at nothing.

If one first gives himself to the Lord, all other giving is easy.

—Robert E. Harris

The smart, charitable person gives until it hurts, except for advice.

If you let God take the foremost, you won't have to worry about the devil taking the hindmost.

Americans spend fifteen times more money gambling than they donate to churches.   —Rev. Denny J. Brale

You can't take your money with you, but you can send it on ahead.

The greatest possession you have is the 24 hours directly in front of you.

He who buries his talent is making a grave mistake.

Rings and jewels are not gifts, but apologies for gifts. The only gift is a portion of thyself.   —Ralph Waldo Emerson

A PASTOR'S
STEWARDSHIP CHECKLIST

BACKGROUND INFORMATION

1. Approximately how many households are in your congregation?

   _____ Households

2. Approximately what percentage of your attenders have started attending within the last five years?

   _____ % of attenders

3. Approximately what percentage of your attenders are:

   Male _____%

   Female _____%

4. Approximately what percentage of your attenders are:

Less than 18 years old	_____%
18-24 years old	_____%
25-39 years old	_____%
40-59 years old	_____%
60-75 years old	_____%
Over 75 years old	_____%
	total=100%

5. Approximately what percentage of your adult attenders (18 and over) have as their highest level of education:

A 4-year college degree or more	_____%
A high school diploma	_____%
Less than a high school diploma	_____%
	total=100%

6. Approximately what percentage of the households in your congregation have annual incomes of:

Under $20,000	_____%
Between $20,000 and $39,999	_____%
Between $40,000 and $59,999	_____%
Between $60,000 and $99,999	_____%
$100,000 or more	_____%
	total=100%

7. Does your congregation sponsor a compassionate ministry center?

___ Yes

___ No

If yes: Is the center self-supporting, or does it require a subsidy?

___ It is self-supporting.

___ It provides a surplus to the congregation: $_____/year.

___ It requires a subsidy: $_____/year.

8. In the past year, has your congregation sponsored or supported anyone involved in:

___ Youth in Mission (YIM)

   Total financial support $_____

___ Work and Witness (W&W)

   Total financial support $_____

___ Other special mission service or project

   Total financial support $_____

9. For the past complete fiscal year, how much money was raised from the following?

Tithes $_____

Missions related giving $_____

Benevolence $_____

Capital campaign (buildings) $_____

Wills, bequests, and special gifts $_____

Investments (including endowments) $_____

Rents and fees $_____

General or district subsides $_____

Other:_____ $_____

10. Does your congregation have an endowment fund?

___ Yes

___ No

If yes: How is the income to be spent? (check only one)

___ General operating budget

___ Capital improvements

___ Special mission or program

___ Other _____

11. Do you use any of the following strategies to encourage lay giving? (For each of the following groups [a through c] check as many items as apply per group and indicate the number of times where asked).

a. Sermons on stewardship:

___ By pastor   _____times/year

___ By laypersons   _____times/year

___ Do not have sermons on stewardship.

b. Appeals or testimonies during worship services:

___ By pastor   _____times/year

___ By laypersons   _____times/year

___ Do not have appeals during worship.

c. Appeals by mail:

___ From the pastor   _____times/year

___ From laypersons   _____times/year

___ Do not have appeals by mail.

STEWARDSHIP AGENCIES

Christian Stewardship Association
Brian Kluth, President
3195 S. Superior
P.O. Box 07747
Milwaukee, WI 53207
414-483-1945
CSA@stewardship.org
Web site: www.stewardship.org

INJOY Stewardship Services
Dave Sutherland, President
P.O. Box 7700
Atlanta, GA 30357-0700
800-333-6509
www.Injoy.com

Raising Money for Your Church
Barna Research Group Ltd.
647 W. Broadway
Glendale, CA 91204-6509

Virgil Hensley, Inc.
6116 E. 32nd St.
Tulsa, OK 74135
918-664-8520

Stewardship Development Ministries
Dr. Steve Weber, Director
6401 The Paseo
Kansas City, MO 64131-1213
800-544-8413
Steward@nazarene.org

Church Growth Institute
Larry Gilbert, President
1-800-553-GROW
Phone for Stewardship Resource Packets by Elmer Towns,
*Tithing Is Christian, God Is Able, Our Family Giving to God's Family,
From Victory to Victory*
These programs were written by Elmer Towns and used at
Thomas Road Baptist Church, Lynchburg, Virginia.

STEWARDSHIP
BIBLIOGRAPHY

Bibliography of Recommended Reading

Alcorn, R. *Money, Possessions and Eternity*. Wheaton, Ill.: Tyndale House Publishers, Inc., 1989.

Barna, G. *How to Increase Giving in Your Church*. Ventura, Calif.: Regal Books, 1997.

Barrett, W. C. *The Church Finance Idea Book*. Nashville: Discipleship Resources, 1993.

Benson, Bob, and Michael W. Benson. *Disciplines for the Inner Life*. Waco, Tex.: Word Books, 1985.

Bergstrom, R. L. In G. Fenton. *Mastering Church Finances*. Portland, Oreg.: Multnomah Press, 1992.

Buford, B. *Half Time*. Grand Rapids: Zondervan Publishing House, 1994.

Crosson, R. *A Life Well Spent*. Nashville: Thomas Nelson, Inc., 1994.

Dayton, H. *Your Money Counts*. Longwood, Fla.: Crown Ministries, 1995.

Dillon, W. P. *People Raising*. Chicago: Moody Press, 1993.

Fisher, Wallace. *A New Climate for Stewardship*. Nashville: Abingdon Press, 1976.

Foster, Richard J. *Freedom of Simplicity*. San Francisco: Harper and Row, 1981.

_____. *Money, Sex, and Power*. San Francisco: Harper and Row, 1985.

Getz, G. A. *A Biblical Theology of Material Possessions*. Chicago: Moody, 1990.

Goodwin, J. W. *Tithing: The Touchstone of Stewardship*. Kansas City: Nazarene Publishing House, n.d.

Hall, Douglas John. *The Steward: A Biblical Symbol Come of Age*. New York: Friendship Press, 1982.

_____. *The Stewardship of Life in the Kingdom of Death*. Grand Rapids: Wm. B. Eerdmans Publishing Co., 1985.

Hoge, D. R. In Wayne Fenton. *Money Matters*. Louisville: Westminster/John Knox Press, 1996.

Nouwen, Henri J. M. *In the Name of Jesus*. New York: Crossroad, 1989.

Perkins, Phyllis H. *The Bible Speaks to Me About My Service and Mission*. Kansas City: Beacon Hill Press of Kansas City, 1990.

Rieke, Thomas C. "Youth Are Stewards," *Clergy Journal*. April 1989.

Salter, Darius. "Our Vocation: Ministry," *Sounding Board*. Summer 1996.

Schaller, L. E. *44 Ways to Expand the Financial Base of Your Congregation*. Nashville: Abingdon Press, 1989.

Smith, Harold Ivan. *The Jabez Principle: A Christian Perspective of Work and Lifestyle*. Kansas City: Beacon Hill Press of Kansas City, 1987.

Spruce, Fletcher C., and James R. Spruce. *You Can Be a Joyful Tither*. Kansas City: Beacon Hill Press of Kansas City, 1985.

Stockton, John. *Investments Here and Hereafter*. Kansas City: Nazarene Publishing House, 1964.

Strait, C. Neil. *Stewardship Is More than Time, Talent, and Things.* Kansas City: Beacon Hill Press of Kansas City, 1993.

Taylor, W. A. *Proving God.* Cleveland: Pathway Press, 1991.

Thompson, Richard Austin. "Stewardship," *Clergy Journal,* July 1991.

Toler, Stan. *Stewardship Starters.* Kansas City: Beacon Hill Press of Kansas City, 1996.

_____. *Stewardship Strategies.* Kansas City: Beacon Hill Press of Kansas City, 1998.

_____. *Stewardship of Time.* Kansas City: Beacon Hill Press of Kansas City, 1998.

Wagner, C. Peter. *Your Spiritual Gifts Can Help Your Church Grow.* Ventura, Calif.: Regal 1979.

Wolf, Earl C. *Tithing Is for Today.* Kansas City: Beacon Hill Press of Kansas City, 1981.

**For books by Elmer Towns and Stan Toler
call Beacon Hill Press of Kansas City
800-877-0700**

NOTES

Introduction

1. John and Sylvia Ronsvalle, *Behind the Stained Glass Windows: Money Dynamic in the Church* (Grand Rapids: Baker Books, 1996), 130.

2. David L. Goetz, *Leadership Journal,* winter 1996, 62.

Chapter 1

1. Waldo J. Werning, *Supply-Side Stewardship* (St. Louis: Concordia Publishing House, 1986), 63.

2. Stuart Briscoe, *Choices for a Lifetime* (Wheaton, Ill.: Tyndale Publishing, 1995), 143.

3. Carl Bangs, *Herald of Holiness,* March 1997.

4. Quoted in *Stewardship Matters Magazine* 1, fall 1997, 17.

5. Dean R. Hoge, *National Contextual Factors Influencing Church Trends: Understanding Church Growth and Decline: 1950-1978,* eds. Dean R. Hoge and David A. Roozen (New York: Pilgrim Press, 1979), 89.

6. Jim Bakker, *I Was Wrong* (Nashville: Thomas Nelson Publishers, 1997), 571.

Chapter 2

1. *Stewardship Matters Magazine* 1, fall 1997.

2. Quoted in John and Sylvia Ronsvalle, *Behind the Stained Glass Windows,* 190.

3. Werning, *Supply-Side Stewardship,* 99.

4. Ibid.

5. *Stewardship Matters Magazine* 17.

6. Ibid.

7. Charles Swindoll, *Laugh Again: Experience Outrageous Joy* (Anaheim, Calif.: Insight for Living, 1992), cassette tape 6-B.

8. Joseph Stowell, *Leadership Journal,* fall 1996, 108.

9. Larry Burkett, *Family Budget Matters* (Wheaton, Ill.: Tyndale House Publishers, 1977), 11.

10. Werning, *Supply-Side Stewardship,* 126.

11. Gary Morsch, *Lay Ministry: It's Not Just for Ministers* (Kansas City: Beacon Hill Press of Kansas City, 1995), 140.

12. Sam Williams, "New Ideas in Church Vitality," *Net Results,* July 1998, 15.

Chapter 3

1. Stan Toler, *The People Principle: Transforming Laypersons into Leaders* (Kansas City: Beacon Hill Press of Kansas City, 1997), 65.

2. Daniel D. Busby, Kent E. Barber, and Robert L. Temple, *The Christian's Guide to Worry-Free Money Management* (Grand Rapids: Zondervan Publishing House, 1994), 47.

3. Toler, *People Principle*, 42.

4. Stan Toler, *Minute Motivators* (Kansas City: Beacon Hill Press of Kansas City, 1996), 62. Used with permission.

Chapter 4

1. Merriam-Webster, *Webster's New Collegiate Dictionary* (Springfield, Mass.: G and C Merriam Company, 1975).

Chapter 5

1. Werning, *Supply-Side Stewardship*, 30.

2. Memo No. 11, Church of the Nazarene, Pensions and Benefits USA (Kansas City).

3. John Wesley, *The Works of Wesley*, Journal (Compact Disc; Boston: Providence House Publishers, 1995), 6:136.

4. Ibid., 1:160.

5. Ibid., 256.

6. Ibid., 349.

7. Ibid., 4:295.

8. See Toler, *People Principle*, 63.

9. Wesley, *Works*, 1:364.

10. Dennis Waitley, *Empires of the Mind* (New York: William Morron and Company, 1995), 6.

Chapter 6

1. Busby et al., *Christian's Guide to Worry-Free Money Management*, 3.

2. Gifts to foundations, public policy groups, environmental groups, and so forth.

3. *The Heart of the Donor* (The Russ Reed Company and Barna Research Group, January 1995), 3.

4. Keith Hinson, *Christianity Today* (April 7, 1997), 58.

5. Larry Burkett, *Your Finances in Changing Times* (Chicago: Moody Press, 1975), 94.

6. *The Heart of the Donor*, 19.

7. C. Neil Strait, *Stewardship Is More than Time, Talent, and Things* (Kansas City: Beacon Hill Press of Kansas City, 1993), 42.